They, Don't Teach You That about Happiness

A Guide for Setting Goals and Creating a Plan to Achieve Them

Jessica Fay-Carrano, LCSW

THEY DON'T TEACH YOU THAT ABOUT HAPPINESS
A GUIDE FOR SETTING GOALS AND
CREATING A PLAN TO ACHIEVE THEM

iUniverse books may be ordered through booksellers or by contacting:

iUniverse
1663 Liberty Drive
Bloomington, IN 47403
www.iuniverse.com
1-800-Authors (1-800-288-4677)

ISBN: 978-1-5320-8527-7 (sc)
ISBN: 978-1-5320-8528-4 (e)

Library of Congress Control Number: 2019916875

Print information available on the last page.

iUniverse rev. date: 11/18/2019

Contents

Acknowledgments

This book would not have been possible without my mom and dad, who were the ones that deeply instilled the belief that all dreams can become a reality if you are willing to work hard and stay dedicated. I am beyond grateful for their unwavering love and support as I have continued to grow as a person through the different seasons of my life.

Thank you to my husband for being my partner in crime on this journey, and for never doubting my ability to do what I have dreamt up in my mind. Without that support and the humor he adds to this world, we would not be where we are today.

I would also like to dedicate this work to my children for giving new learning and growing opportunities every minute of every day, and for allowing me to truly practice what I preach as I try to lead by example for them both to find their happiness in this life.

Preface

Who the Heck Am I

Welcome to the beginning of looking at life in a whole new way. I'm honored that you would take the time to learn something new and work to better yourself and your life, and allow me to be a part of this journey. If there is one thig that I have learned through my career as a licensed clinical social worker (you know, a therapist), as well as through my personal experiences, it is that being grateful for every moment and experience will fill you with all the positivity and motivation you will need to get out of bed every day and tackle whatever you put on your to-do list.

Let me be clear with my definition of "positivity" because I feel that this word has been getting a bad rap over the past few years. Most people have come to think of positivity as the process of disregarding all the negative and hard pieces of our lives. Similar to the old saying about putting on rose-colored glasses, people think that that in order to be positive you must ignore that life throws some pretty tough and large obstacles our way for us to tackle. I believe that being a positive thinker is more about recognizing these negative pieces, large and small, and still identifying that good exists in the world and in tough situations as well. We then make the choice to focus on the positive and where this will lead us. This is not done to disregard the negative; it is done intentionally in the pursuit of happiness and balance. Yes, awful things happen and exist in the world, and they will continue to do so until the end of time. We have no control over that. What we can control is what we choose to use our time focusing on and what the outcome will be in our lives despite, and in light of, the fact that the negative and difficult pieces are part of the reality. I believe that this is the core component needed to be able to make the mind-set shift that is necessary to make change in our lives.

I didn't always buy into that, or at least I was not as aware that this was the process my brain used to get me from milestone to milestone. It sounded a little too touchy-feely for my liking when the actual concepts that encompass this were presented to me in school through my education as a social worker. That's one thing to know about me. I'm a therapist that, when focusing on feelings, is much less "How does that make you feel?" and more "Let's discuss the science behind how our emotions are chemical reactions in our body created by the stimuli in our environment through our senses, and that we can control the impact of our emotions being created by controlling our cognitions." Yup, I'm more of a science geek than I would usually openly admit. This also holds true in my view about being action oriented. You will find throughout my strategies that I am looking at where we are at any given moment. I am less concerned about how we get to where we are (as in the cause-and-effect view), and more concerned about where are we right now and where we are going next. Yet here I am, telling you that I believe in positive thinking and being grateful for the millions upon millions of tiny miracles that happen every day, both great and challenging.

So why the mind shift? I mean, I obviously had the theoretical background from grad school to back up the emotional thinking part. At the time I attended, NYU was known as one of the best clinical social work schools in the United States, and I received a boatload of knowledge to perfect the "How does that make you feel?" part of being a social worker. The funny part about that is that I still cannot, to this day, pull off that sentence without the person that hears it at least cracking a smile—and usually laughing. If we ever get to meet, ask me to say it for you. I guarantee it will make your day a little brighter with the humor and irony of it. So it's a little tricky to lead with this. Plus, I have always had more of an interest—no, really a passion—for the "And then what?"—you know, what comes next. For me it's more about the here and now, and less about the cause. Let's say we meet for years to discuss everything about the past to figure out why your favorite color is purple. It's all well and good if we figure out the root cause, yet where does that leave you? It has done nothing to change what you are doing now; nor have we figured out what needs to be done to make something different. This is the "And then what?" This also allows us to take ownership for our situation, as well as all of our thoughts, emotions, and actions in that situation. We will come back to why this is so amazing, yet so challenging, later.

In retrospect, I realized that anytime I achieved something monumental prior to gaining this knowledge formally through education, it was when I was focused on the "And then what?" I think the reason I did not actually know this was the case was that I naturally made decisions about what these next steps would be. This was mainly because I am a person that thinks in this manner and gathers all the information to make a decision. Let's look at my journey into social work.

To my memory, I had never met a social worker in my life when

I chose to become one. I'm sure I had, but I do not recall ever having a conversation with someone who explained what a social worker did or what the field had to offer someone. Hollywood and television do not really do a great job giving my chosen profession a glamorous look either, so I truly had no clue about this world I am now a part of. In high school, the big questions on the table were, of course, "What do you want to be when you grow up?" and "Where are you going to college?" Like the good rule-follower I am, I wanted to have an answer to these questions. Cue the information-gathering journey.

I knew that I liked to help people, as when someone needed information or needed a resource, it made me feel good to be the one to provide what was needed. In high school and college, I worked in retail, and I was not only the first person to volunteer to help customers in the store but also loved to give directions to the closest restaurant or a place where they could get the best deal on something they were looking for. I loved to search out and share information and connect people to what they needed. So, without formally labeling it, I set a goal to find a profession that would allow me to do this. I started doing research on the field of psychology, which seemed to be a close fit, but I continued to dig. This was where I found social work programs. It appeared that I could do so much more with a social work degree that would align with what I loved to do than with any other degree. Now I had an answer to the first question. Now I needed to find a program to attend that offered a degree in my field of choice and was close to home.

Through this search, I discovered that there was a way to obtain a master's in social work in a year by attending an undergraduate program that was part of the accredited program and then being accepted to the master's program with advanced standing. This would save me time and money, so I was sold. I applied to programs that would allow me to do this, which led me to spend four years at Sacred Heart University for undergrad, and a year at New York University for graduate school. I remember having a moment my junior year of undergrad when I realized that I had never really thought about other options after high school. I could have continued to just work, or maybe travel. For me, I had set the goal to become a social worker, and in order to do that, I needed to pursue a master's degree, so that's what I did. I wanted to save time and money, so I went for the most cost- and time-effective option available. I had already started to understand that I needed to identify what I wanted specifically, and it needed to be something I felt passionate about. Then I could identify what would be necessary to make it happen, and start moving toward it. I chose to attend NYU not just because they were one of the best schools but also because I loved the environment I would get to learn in and from, and because they gave me a scholarship.

I already knew I did not want to live in New York after graduation, so I did not think it was a good use of time and money to live there. So, without much thought, I worked with the university to be able to take all my classes on one day and do my internship in Connecticut, which was where I lived. My focus was on building relationships and my career where I planned to reside, so I had to find a way to make that happen while I attended the school of my choice. My first class every Thursday for two fifteen-week semesters started at 8:00 a.m. I would take the 5:40 a.m. train into the city and would finish with my classes right before 7:00 p.m. I would sprint to the subway to get back to Grand Central to take the express train so I could be home almost thirty minutes sooner than if I had to take the next train. When I reflect on this, it still feels surreal that this was my life for a year. Add in a retail job three days a week and a three-day-a-week internship. I did all of this because that was what was necessary to get to where I wanted to go. The "And then what?" pushed me past the negativity of the early mornings, cold weather, long days, and hard work that was being put in. I share this story, and all of the stories that follow, not as an opportunity to brag or send a message that I am better than anyone. First of all, I believe that we are all our own individual selves that have the potential to achieve whatever we set our minds to and are willing to put in the hard work toward achieving. This will be different for everyone; that's the whole point of this book and of life in general. We get to decide where we want to go and what we want to achieve, and if we are willing to try and work hard toward it, we will achieve it. That is the purpose of the stories I share—to show that things are possible if we put our heads in the right place and work toward each step through the process.

Focusing on the "And then what?" is where I have learned the most about myself. I have had this belief reinforced by having had the opportunity to be part of countless people's journeys into figuring out their "And then what?" This is where the goal for writing this book comes from. My journey has led me to a place of wanting to be able to share my experience and expertise with the masses to allow all people to have the skills that will allow them to achieve the most happiness in their lives that they can. I still love and believe in the personal interaction and individualized journey that providing therapy offers and creates. I also believe that therapy will be an essential tool of some people's journeys. There are also a large number of people that may hesitate to have this be a piece of their journey through life. Therapy has become more commonly accepted in some parts of society, but there is still a misconception as to what therapy can be and is, not to mention the struggle most people have around the idea of asking for help or needing help in general. I had a conversation that led me to think about how to repackage the benefits of therapy that would potentially appeal to more people and, in turn, allow more people to reap the benefits of the services I offer. The best way I could think to do this was through a published book. So here it is. Here is my attempt at giving a summary and overview of what I have used to project my life forward, and I continue to collaborate with many people to do the same.

I am guessing that since you are an intelligent individual, you may be asking yourself about my journey, which I have briefly mentioned. You may be curious about what experiences I had that led me from being a new clinical social worker fresh out of grad school to wanting to write a book to inspire the world. When I say it like that, I understand that it's kind of a big jump. Since I did not set out to write a memoir, at this point I won't bore you with all the details of over a decade, but I will give you a few examples that were big light bulb moments for me—the moments when, looking back, I could truly say I was a changed person, especially after my formal training, when I had more of a clue about how to structure my life and challenge myself to grow personally and professionally. If you are not interested in my personal journey or examples, or if you are ready to get started working on your journey, that's great! Please feel free to skip to the next chapter!

Typically for me, these light bulb moments also have been times after which I have felt hypocritical, since the experience changed my outlook completely. One example of this occurred when I was pregnant with my first child, my daughter, and feeling super proud of how far I had come in my career in a short time. I was talking about my glorious return from maternity leave to continue to pursue my career and dedicate myself to the people our program served. Within hours of her being born, I made the announcement that I would be leaving my job to watch my daughter sleep and to be with her all day long. This is not actually how that story ended up playing out, but I can totally understand why parents want to stay home with their children, career or not. For the record, I also understand why parents return to work also. I just didn't think the former applied to me—until it did. This was one of the first times that I had really veered away from the plan of my life in some major way. It was uncomfortable for this girl that lives for a plan. I struggle without a plan, and I used to really struggle when the plan went off course.

I still don't love when the plan takes a detour, but I am grateful that I rebound and regroup more quickly than I used to. This is thanks to the experiences that have pushed me through struggle to strength as of late. This was one of those times. I did indeed return to work, after giving my resignation on the Thursday before my birthday. As I write that, I take a pause to realize that my birthday was the next day, a Friday, which would be another impactful day six years later. But back to work. The following Monday, my employer contacted me to ask what I would consider doing, because they did not want to lose me. We set a time to meet, and they worked to create a part-time position that allowed me to use the strengths I have while providing me the extra time with my daughter I wanted. This lasted for a year, until the funding for the position was no longer available and I had to decide to stay and go back to full-time or leave and count on my backup plan of building my private practice. Because I had not clearly defined my goal of happiness at this point, I made the easier and safer choice to stay at the agency. A few years later, I was promoted, and to be honest, that was when shit got real for me. I stuck it out until I hated crying almost every day, having a knot in my shoulder, and suffering from a twitch in my eye, all from stress, enough to say, "I won't do this to myself anymore." The completing factor to this occurred on that Friday, on my birthday six years after my first resignation. But let me explain another light bulb moment that happened first, so you can get a clear picture of the path I walked.

Let's fast-forward from my daughter's birth to my being pregnant with my son. I wanted to have a "leave me alone until there is a problem or a baby is coming out" natural birth. This is easier said than done when you have had a C-section prior in most areas of the country. Before I carry on with my story, let me state for the record that I believe in a woman's right to choose how she gives birth. You want a natural birth? Go for it. You want a C-section? Schedule it. You want all the pain medication available? Start taking it. This is not a "you should want this too because my experience was amazing for me" story. This is an "I'm going to do something I always swore I would never do" story, because this is the story of how we decided to have my son at home, in a birthing tub in my bedroom. I did this for no reason other than that I was so focused on giving birth to my son the way I wanted to. Here's a little more of the backstory so it makes a little more sense, because I get that, for most people, that seems like an extreme leap.

I started off my pregnancy with the same providers I used for my daughter's pregnancy and delivery, who also happen to be my regular OB-GYN providers. Since I had a C-section with my daughter, I knew I would need to educate myself more on labor and delivery than I had during my daughter's pregnancy. One of my coping strategies when I am faced with a barrier is to "learn all the things." So I jumped down the rabbit hole of VBAC, meaning "vaginal birth after cesarean." This was when I became overwhelmed with the information about how difficult it is for some women, depending on the provider, hospital one delivers in, etc. to achieve this. And forget about doing so free of intervention. This rabbit hole led me also to take a specific birthing class that used strategies like affirmations and relaxation techniques for an easier, calmer labor and delivery. It was also the place where Mike and I were exposed to home birthing with clear statistics and evidence of the safety medical soundness for both the mother and the child.

After the monthlong class was over, I scheduled my next appointment with a specific doctor that I knew would be up front about how my labor and delivery would play out at our local hospital. To sum up the visit, he told me that while he was extremely impressed with how healthy of a person I was and with my ability to advocate for myself, his concern was that I would have to spend the whole labor advocating for my rights and wishes, and that seemed contrary to what I was trying to achieve. I am still beyond grateful for this visit—not because I left happy, because I was in tears—but because of his honesty. When I came home, Mike didn't need to ask how it had gone because I still had a bad face on. He just said, "Let's buy a blow-up pool and have the baby right here in the bedroom. If that's what you want to do, and it will make you happy, then that's what we do." So less than three months before my due date, we made an appointment with a midwife group that a childhood friend recommended after she used them for her home birth, and we switched providers. Fast-forward several weeks, and after only about five hours of labor I delivered my chunky baby boy in my bedroom. The first thought I had when I scooped him up was "I did it!" Quickly after, I thought "He's so chubby!" But that's a different story. This was the moment I had visualized every night before I went to sleep, and that I had described for people when they asked about my plans for birthing, and it is the one that still makes me well up when I talk about it.

You see, when you are so specific on that goal, the outcome you visualize that sets your heart and soul on fire, you will do whatever is necessary to get there. Sometimes you will even do things others will judge you for, and things you always said were outside of something you would ever consider doing. These are both brief examples of light bulb moments that led to stepping outside of the plan to grow and try on a new cognition—not because it was easy or comfortable, but because it was worth it.

So in both of these situations, there were choices involved. These were not situations of crisis for me; nor was I in them completely involuntarily. Sometimes life throws us major curveballs that throw the plan all out of whack, and we can get stuck in that. I may not have completely made the jump from my agency-based job to self-employment through my private practice as I initially intended when I had my daughter, but I did several years later. Life decided that I needed another growing opportunity to really push me to a new place.

On my birthday, a Friday in 2018 that was six years after my first resignation, my father called me bright and early. My dad is not a phone person. He doesn't call to chat or make small talk. There is a purpose to his calls, so I was initially nervous. He normally went into work early, and he knows I get up early to get my workout in, so then I pushed my thoughts to consider that he was actually calling to say happy birthday. Sometimes our instincts really are in tune with the universe, because he was calling not to wish me a happy birthday but to tell me that my younger sister had passed away. She was my only sibling, and younger than me by nine and a half years. She was the reason that I became known as "Sissy," which I am still known as to most people in my personal life. There is so much I can say about her, who she was as a person, and her incredible spirit. But I will stick to the messages that I continue to take away from this as I still work through it all.

During the months after she passed, I realized that I was going to have to really practice what I had been preaching all these years. I needed to set some big, scary goals to really get me excited to get out of bed every morning to be the best version of me in all the roles I filled. I needed to stop crying every day because of stress, I needed time to process my loss and be present to support my family in doing the same, and I needed to find a way to bring back that fire in my belly that pushed me to be the best version of me I could be. I wanted to live up to the words that I spoke at her funeral when I said how proud I was to be her sister, and I wanted her to be proud of me as her sister too. So I made the leap into self-employment, which led to the conversation I mentioned about how to further my reach into the world, and then I decided to write this book, using my journey to support others in their quests for happiness and to further my own similar quest as a guide to utilize these skills I had been teaching so many other people to use to change their lives.

I searched out the information I needed to understand what would need to be possible for me to do this, and I sought out the tools, support, and education to get myself there. I continued to learn along the way to better prepare myself and not hold myself back from starting by having the excuse that this was an area I knew very little about. As excited as I was about making the leap, I was scared out of my mind. Change comes with entering into the unknown, which will always frighten us. I also knew that I was ready to face that challenge and that I was done trying to find ways to cope with my current hard situation. If I wanted something different and something better for myself, the time to make the leap into the unknown was now. Again, it is not always easy to get started, and it is always scary to keep going, but please believe me; it can be so worth it. You are worth it! How can I say that without ever having met you? I am confident that if you have taken the time to read even this far, you have the inner strength and desire to have something different, and better, in your life. Each one of us has the right and the ability to decide what makes us happy and makes this life worth living. This is not accomplished at another person's discomfort or unhappiness, and it is not done without the regard of others. This is about having us be the starting point, and deciding how we get there within ourselves.

There is a difference between not caring about what others will think and say, and doing and saying things that we know will offend and hurt others. We start with ourselves and our own desires, and then we can consider others and plan for those potential barriers so that we can still get to where we want to be. This journey is different for everyone, since we are all created with our own unique sets of strengths and challenges. We are all here to face up to the challenges ahead, put in the hard work, and celebrate the successes along the way. Each time we achieve something, there will be a new challenge to overcome, which in turn will give us a new learning opportunity and a new success to celebrate. This process will lead individuals to become different types of people, such as billionaires, Olympic athletes, veterinary hospital managers, published authors, schoolteachers, and owners of successful metal fabrication shops. The possibilities are different for each of us, and each is as important as the others, since its path represents the life each person is living. It is the responsibility of each of us to decide to follow the specific path we choose to see how far we can go. This book will hopefully serve as a guide on that journey toward whatever it is you decide to achieve and create the commitment and consistency necessary to make it a reality.

The Power of Setting Goals

We all have a superpower. Every single person on this planet has his or her very own superpower; it is the power to decide how he or she will live his or her life. This is one of those things that no one really takes the time to truly teach us. While it is true that we do not always have control over what happens around us in the world, we do have the ability to decide how we will feel and think about it, and in turn how we will act upon it moving forward. Yet most people live out their lives without ever knowing that they have this ability, and even more people have heard of this but have never really been taught or mastered the skills to put it into practice.

Just like any great superhero story, each one of our stories will start with struggles in life that lead to the discovery of the superpower we possess. Most people get stuck in the beginning part of their story with their struggles. We get caught up in trying to push through without understanding how to heal and how to deal with these struggles. We do not take the time to gain the knowledge necessary to develop a plan that will allow us to achieve the things we desire from life. We treat happiness as a destination, as a place we can reach, and until we reach it, we will suffer and be miserable. We view other people in the world who appear to be happy, and we decide that it was meant for them and not us, or we tell ourselves that they must be being deceitful and are just really great liars. We have not been taught to stop and turn inward to understand how we are feeling and what we think, and then assess how this affects our actions during every moment of every day.

Even if we make the beginning efforts to gain this knowledge, it may seem overwhelming and difficult to understand, and even more difficult to apply and put into practice. This is my effort to give you a comprehensive guide to all the things no one has taught us about goal-setting and about achieving our version of happiness. These are the skills I have worked to build with countless others to make goal-setting an essential piece of life, as well as a manageable task and skill.

Whether you are interested in something as small as wanting to have a plan to remember what groceries you need to buy when you go to the grocery store, or something as large as changing careers to start your own business making the most delicious cupcakes the world has ever tasted, this guide and the skills that you will build by working through it will support you in achieving what you set out to achieve, as well as decreasing the amount of time it takes you to achieve it. I can promise that it will not be easy, since no good self-realization story ever is, yet it will be worth it if you decide it is important enough to try.

So often we tackle a problem in our life from the wrong side. We identify that we have something in our lives that we would like to change or be different. For example, we might say, "I hate my job," "I'm overweight and tired all of the time," or "My partner is a pain in the ass and doesn't listen to me or help me out in any way." You get the point. We then try to figure out to where to start. (Insert positive motivational quote.) We feel super inspired to do something different. So we jump right in. We start to think about what we can do first to get started. Then we think of all the other steps that might be necessary. We then slowly (or sometimes pretty quickly) begin losing the motivation and momentum we almost had going. Now we really get in our own way and start identifying all the barriers to the steps we just identified. (Cue the sad background music.) The job hunt halts, and we are on the couch with the gallon of ice cream, watching the next two seasons of the show we are binge-watching, while our partner does whatever he or she wants (which is still not the laundry or dishes to help us out). Heck, we will probably have a fight with our partner just to really drive home the belief that nothing can ever change. Our brains are so helpful in that way.

Our brains will create and search out any cognition and belief that supports the direction in which we are headed. That is not so helpful in the above scenario. When we believe that nothing will change, we are right. When we believe that change sucks and is hard, we are right. Yet when we believe that we are capable of change and that something better is waiting for us around the corner, we are just as right as we are in the other examples. We just need to choose what we want to add or subtract from our life, and we need to know why this is so important and what components we can identify that will try to get in our way. This is where our power lies—in the moment when we deliberately decide what our focus will be. When we identify something that we want to be different in our lives, we must first start at the finish line in our minds. What do I want to achieve? What will

3

it look like? Answering these questions will help your mind start to focus on the positive outcome and develop the goal. From here we then move to the why. Why do I want this change so badly? Why is it so important? This will continue to reinforce the positive while creating a motivation that will allow you to be ruthless in your consistency to do whatever it takes to kick ass in working toward your goal. Next we can develop the road map of steps that we will need to take in order to achieve the change we desperately need and want. Now, don't go jumping back to the starting line again just yet. We are still standing at the finish. Starting from this vantage point allows us to reverse engineer our steps to utilize our positive mind-set to plan not only for the steps necessary but also for the barriers that may pop up. This makes it much more likely we will complete each step and tackle each barrier as it presents itself. Once this is all mapped out, we can step up to the starting line, take our marks, get set, and *go!*

Sounds easy, right? *Wrong!* Let's still be honest that this will still be hard. We are biologically programmed to resist and fear change. I mean, change is different, and our brains like to be able to predict what's around the next corner. This was an instinct that served us well back in the days when we all lived in caves. It kept us from getting eaten if we stayed on the paths that we knew were safe, and from getting poisoned by eating only the berries on the familiar bush. We can thank nature for kicking in here. We can pair this with the ever-so-helpful beliefs that we have about ourselves. We can dig deeper into some of these in more detail later, so let's just label these the thoughts we have about ourselves that we tell ourselves over and over that make us believe we are not good enough.

I have to let you in on a little secret that you may not be aware of. All of these thoughts of self-doubt that we have were taught to us. We were not born with them. Someone in our life planted the seeds, and we worked with them to water and grow the snarling vines they have become today. This also means that we have the power to get the pruning shears and trowel out to cut back and remove any belief and thought that will not serve us the way we want it to. So let's take a moment to appreciate where all this anxiety and discomfort is stemming from. And now let's move on from it.

Although this is the reason we have these thoughts, that does not mean we have to let it be our excuse. We can override this if we are willing to put in the hard work of continuing to bring our thoughts and intentions back to the belief that something can and will be different. We will need to take a leap of faith, which is just choosing to believe in something we are not sure exists—choosing to just try. Once we go down this rabbit hole together of challenging the way we view our ability to utilize our emotions, thoughts, and behaviors to change our perspective on life, we will not be disappointed. We can all celebrate that we are no longer striving to reach the end point of this journey to achieve happiness, however we each individually define that at any point in time. We will become travelers on the journey through life, acknowledging and experiencing the happiness that is the journey itself.

Disclaimer

I believe in transparency. I believe in the importance of being as honest as I can at any point in time. This means I share and explain things to the best of my ability based on my current understanding and perspective. Because of this, you may get tired of how often I bring up how hard this process of setting and achieving goals is. This may not sound super motivational, but at least it's honest. And if we are on this journey together, we will need to be honest. So here's the deal: I will be honest with you. And you will need to be honest with yourself. This is the platform from which we can tackle the hard things together. Even though this process of changing is hard because of the fear and unpredictability of the unknown, let's be honest; it's just as hard to continue to live exactly the same way you are living now. That's why you are reading this book. This is why you have thought about wanting to make a change. The situation you are in may be familiar, but it is also hard. So pick your challenge. The issue you face will continue to stay the same or get worse. But pushing through the difficulty of the unknown will get you something different. This is where the potential for greatness, your greatness, lies. You just have to pick this option. We will start by creating and writing down our goals, and then we will learn to implement a framework to identify potential barriers and supports to being able to implement the plan we will create. So, if you are still ready to push on with me into difficult terrain, let's break out each step of effective goal-setting to prepare you to start living the life you deserve and can achieve.

The What

First we need to decide what our goal will be. This seems like the simple part, right? "I want to lose weight." "I want to make more money." "I want to be happy." Done. Moving on to part two. Um, yeah. Not so much. Let's back up. While these statements may give us a general idea of the area we want to focus on, they are exactly that—general, and just areas of focus. When we set goals that are too broad and general, everything else that comes after that will feel the same way, and when we develop steps that are too general and broad, they seem consuming and unattainable—not exactly the setup for success we are looking for. So we need to start getting very specific with what it is we want. When deciding on what your goal will be, take a few minutes to really sit and focus on it. Visualize what your life will be like when you reach the goal. What is different? How do you look and feel in your visualization? How far in the future have you gone when you achieve this? What are you doing? Capture all the specifics and write them down. This will turn your general goal of "I will make more money" into something like "I will make an extra $60,000 this year that will allow me to take my family on our dream vacation to Barbados and stay in that resort I saw the commercial for on YouTube for one week to celebrate my birthday." Boom! This can be a goal to get excited about! Picture all the delicious food you will eat each day, the activities you can plan and enjoy, the color of the water, the sand between your toes, the smiles on the faces of your family members, and the flavor of the cake when they sing "Happy Birthday to You" while you are wearing that fabulous designer outfit you spied while window-shopping the other day. The more specific you can be, the better.

A goal about losing weight or being healthier sounds like a great one. When does taking better care of oneself sound like a bad idea? The tricky part is that we will have no idea how to go about this when our goal is this general. If we add in details about how to visualize the goal, such as losing twenty pounds, decreasing two pant sizes, being able to walk up the three flights of stairs without being winded, being able to play basketball with our kid for twenty minutes, decreasing our cholesterol number, avoiding developing diabetes, or being able to do twenty pull-ups, it's a lot easier to know where we are trying to move. It also allows others supporting our process to know what we are striving for so they are less likely to give unhelpful feedback. If we tell our best friend that we are trying to lose weight when we are truly just trying to cut out processed sugar, he or she may comment on every little thing we consume. It is not the best way to feel positive when we already turned down the donut at the breakfast meeting, the cake for the coworker at lunch, and the piece of chocolate sitting on the receptionist's desk as we left the building to meet our friend, and all we wanted was to share the meat-and-cheese platter at dinner with him or her. Being specific lets everyone get on the same page, not to mention that this will allow you to really anchor into the specifics of what you are striving for and allow you to more smoothly move into the next phases of the goal-setting process.

I will advise that the initial outline of your plan should be handwritten, and then you can get creative with how you fine-tune it. Perhaps you can create a flow chart or a to-do list, or you can utilize images to represent each step that you are going to take. This will vary from person to person, and even from goal to goal for the same person. I start by writing out my goal with pen and paper. I usually prefer a good-quality pen in a fun color, and lined paper because, you know, the handwriting. I will take the time to create something, such as an image of my goal, that I can easily access, such as the wallpaper on my phone, or sticky notes placed in various places where I will see them regularly throughout the day. Again, be creative about where you place your reminders. If you look at your phone or computer throughout the day, set your wallpaper to something relevant to your goal or set an alarm to go off at different times regularly so the goal is constantly being brought to the forefront of your mind.

Goals do not always have to be something so huge that they take months or years to achieve. Sometimes the best way to start is small and short-term. This will set us up for success and help us start to challenge any negative beliefs we may have about our ability to achieve anything. This is also helpful during times when we know that something needs to change because we are not happy, yet we are not quite sure where to start or what our goal should be. Asking ourselves what would be different if we felt happy will usually cue us in to what specific area to start in, and then we can pick one specific thing to focus on. To go back to the health goal, maybe we can identify that we want to increase our sleep, so we set a goal to get at least eight hours of sleep, or we may choose to focus on water intake and commit to drinking a half ounce of water per pound of body weight daily for a week. This gives us something very small and short-term to focus on. We can even shorten it to a day just to drive the point home to our brains that yes, we can achieve something if we decide to.

For example, in the moment after I hung up the phone with my dad on my birthday when my sister passed, I had a choice. I had to decide to completely fall apart, which I did for a few minutes, and then I made the conscious choice to set a goal to make it through the day. I quickly outlined what needed to happen. I did this not just in my head, but out loud to Mike as well. My daughter was so excited the night before that it would be my birthday when she woke up, and I wanted to still give that to her. Plus, she needed to go to school. So I broke down the morning routine for Mike and left to go to my parents' house a few miles away, wearing some combination of my workout clothes and pajamas. For the record, I never said that achieving your goals would always be glamourous. I spent some time there and was back home in time to help her get ready for school and to take the ride for school drop-off, which I have done 99.9 percent of the days both my kids have attended school. It's just something that is important to me. I still needed to stick to my plan to feel that I was making progress toward my goal.

So Mike, our son, and I took the thirty-minute drive to our vet to drop off the urine sample from our chocolate lab that needed to be tested that day to ensure she was all set with her antibiotics. It seems crazy to say that's what I did, but that was the agenda for the day, so I stuck with it. Then I told Mike to go to work, and my son and I went to my parents'. Along the same way of thinking, my mom and I went to a store to pay her bill that was due that day. No sense in getting a late charge, right? We were all focused on getting through the day. We stuck together to keep ourselves moving. We reached out to the people we needed to share our news with. We referred to this as "the happy train." We were just spreading the good word for all our loved ones to hear. It's one of those things that are funny because they're true, and if you don't laugh, you will just cry. Later that day, I picked up my daughter from school, as I usually do, and we went home and celebrated my birthday with the gifts she had told Mike to get me. There were cupcakes involved, and they were delicious. We spend Fridays at the rink for ice skating, so off we went. We went out to dinner with my in-laws afterward, as previously planned, because to my daughter and to me, it was important that it still be my birthday.

I told her about her auntie the next morning, but I still feel that I accomplished my goal of making it through that first day. Sure, I cried the ugly cry every moment my kids were out of eyesight, but I stuck to the plan I had created for myself. Then I did the same thing the next day. Over time, I became able to go back to focusing on more than the minute or day in front of me. This is a great reminder that it doesn't always matter whether the goal is very short-term or whether it will take a decade to accomplish; nor does it matter what the payoff of that goal is. Any goal that brings joy and happiness to your life and makes you better is worth setting and achieving. I have no idea how my daughter will view this day when she realizes that the date on my sister's headstone is my birthday and that I didn't tell her until the day after, but that is for her to decide. I made that choice from a place of love, wanting to allow her the joy of having it be her mom's birthday.

When I got the idea to write a book, I took some time to really think about the goal I was envisioning. It was less about my love and talent for writing, and more about the experience I wanted to create for the reader through my words. I wanted to receive feedback from my readers about staying up until all hours of the night because they could not put the book down. I wanted to hear about times when they threw the book down and got to work on their goal journey because they felt so inspired. I wanted to be the one they went back to when they got stuck and the journey was hard, with my words getting them back on the path. I wanted to create opportunities for people to reach their own version of happiness. This was not only reinforced in the therapy I was providing at the time; it was reinforced anytime I walked by a person without a smile, or anytime I read a post on social media about someone going to a job he or she hated, or how stressful life felt for someone and how impossible everything felt for him or her. I wanted to create tools and support that could reach people to give them what they needed to take life to the next level. So I set out to create my plan for achieving this goal of making a positive impact on each person I could come into contact with.

Thank you again for taking the time to join me in my journey, and start yours with me. Here's your chance to get started! Write down your *what*. I have provided extra space below where you can start with a few key points or ideas you want to include. Draft a few versions until the one that really speaks to what you want to strive toward is created.

My What:

_____
_____
_____
_____
_____
_____
_____
_____
_____
_____
_____
_____
_____
_____
_____
_____
_____
_____

The Why

So now you have written (and hopefully rewritten, and broken down several times, and rewritten again) the goal that you are pretty fired up about. Here's an important question: Why do you want to achieve this goal? I mean, why did this even pop into your mind? Why bother taking the time to visualize to exhaustion of this area of your life, and what would be different about it with the achievement of the goal? There will be some key pieces that jump out at you. And at the risk of sounding redundant, as you look at these whys, start getting specific.

The *why* is the component that is the most important aspect of your life currently. This *why* needs to take the jittery, excited feeling you have about your goal and blow it up. I am talking flashing lights, fireworks, and balloons! Create all the feels! It should be something so important to you that when you really focus on it and talk about it, you can feel the tears. If you are by yourself, you do the ugly cry. You know the cry I mean—the one when you make all the bad faces, you make the noise, your body convulses, and you have body fluids coming out of your orifices.

Working out to be able to keep up with your kid on the basketball court for twenty minutes sounds great, but without focusing on the *why*, I bet we will quickly move to a place where being on the sidelines cheering will suffice when the alarm goes off at 5:30 a.m. for your workout call and your bed is super cozy and it's dark and probably cold, so clearly hitting snooze is a better option. This is when we need our *why* the most—when it gets tough. And we already know that it will, firstly because I already told you it would (you're welcome), and secondly because if it were easy you would already have done it. So let's dig deep into why playing basketball with your kid is so important to you. Maybe you want to teach your kid how important it is to work hard for what one wants because he or she is trying out for a team for the first time, or maybe his or her other parent is physically unable to play with him or her, or maybe the basketball court is the only place your kid currently feels proud of himself or herself and you want to encourage and nurture these moments because this world is so cruel. See it in your mind. Hear the sounds and the conversations. Feel the emotions (and, in this example, probably sweat) dripping from you. This is what will get you to throw back the covers and get dressed instead of hitting snooze. Focusing on why you want to achieve your goal, on what it means to you at your core, will always get you further than focusing on just the specific task at hand or all the things we have to do to achieve the goal.

As with creating my *what*, I will also use a similar strategy for my *why*. I will set aside time to reflect and visualize my *why* for the current goal starting. I ensure that this is part of my early-morning and before-bed routines. Always set your intentions for the day by reflecting on your goal, your *why*, and the steps you are taking throughout the day as outlined by your road map. Then end the day with a positive reflection of your goal and your *why*, and make an evaluation of how the steps went. What did you accomplish, how did it go, what did you learn, and what will be needed for the next day to continue to make progress?

Here's an example to highlight the difference of moving from "what" to "why." When I set the goal to write this book, I spent a lot of time focusing on my *why*. It started with my kids. I wanted to create a legacy for them to see and think, "Wow! Our mom is more amazing than we thought. She dedicated her life to helping others improve theirs. How can we strive to become the best versions of ourselves and live the happiest lives possible for ourselves? We can't wait to figure it out and get going!" I also know this will be balanced with all of the other wonderful thoughts and statements that children make about and to their parents, so really I am still striving for balance here. So while this part of my *why* may be more long-term, I can also visualize how that would look in the here and now.

I knew that writing this book would also allow me to be more present with them and purposeful with the time I would get to spend with them. Small things for me are sometimes the most important. These include being able to volunteer on a weekly basis in my children's school, being the one to pick them up on most days, and being able to attend all their sporting and prosocial activities without having to be distracted by a phone or technology. I knew that my writing this book could allow us the freedom to do things as a family without the time or financial burden that may have existed if I were still working for the agency. To be honest, when I am focused on the principles in this book and applying myself to continuing to grow personally to be able to write about these principles, I am far happier and more fun to be around on a daily basis. This is the parallel process I am trying to create. The very idea of creating and teaching purposeful balance in life energizes me more than walking outside with my dogs in the frigid New England winter morning after an intense workout. This then leads me to also spend a great deal of time at different points of the book's journey visualizing my readers (so you, really). I think of the stories I will get to hear about how other people have newfound happiness or quality of life because of support I was able to offer, and how they are paying this forward by leading by example and showing others that it is possible. So thank you for being part of my *why* on this journey of mine. Thank you for allowing me to use the time I spend growing for myself and my loved ones, to help you do the same for you and yours! What will your motivation and driving reasons be to take on the big, scary change you have set as a goal?

Let's start creating a list of things that will be essential in your why statement. Just as with your *what*, it may take a few tries and drafts to get there. This speaks to how important this is—not only in the process but also to you! I usually require tissues during this step.

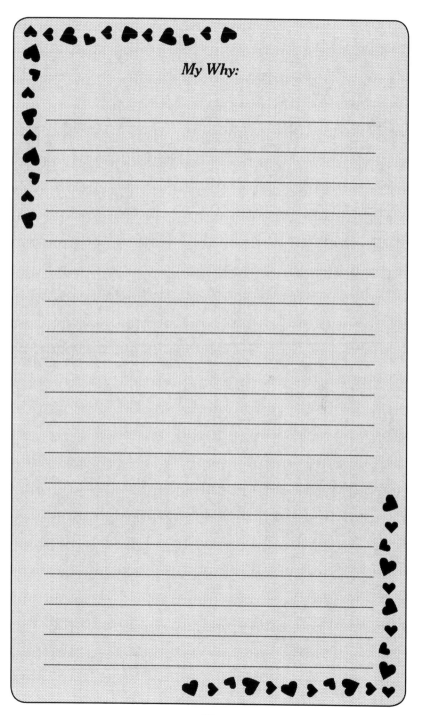

My Why:

_____

_____

_____

_____

_____

_____

_____

_____

_____

_____

_____

_____

_____

_____

_____

_____

_____

_____

The Road Map

Now that we have created our clearly defined goal and fueled it with the most uplifting and meaningful reasons to achieve the goal, let's plan for liftoff. What will be necessary to reach that goal? We need to start from the finish line and work our way backward so as not to get caught up in how daunting and impossible it all may seem and not to get so stuck behind all the potential barriers that will creep up along the way. There will still be plenty of obstacles to compete with, but no worries; I have some helpful tips for those on deck.

Back to our plan. Creating a visual representation of our plan, or road map, allows us to go back to it over time through our journey. So while we will try to be as specific as we can in the steps, we still need to leave some room for flexibility as the plan unfolds. It is also a well-known fact that recording something in some way is the best way to ensure that we remember it, understand it, and are committed to it. So write this stuff down! It increases the chances you will meet the goal. Let's start out with the scale tipped in our favor. As someone with less-than-perfect penmanship (it has been a running joke throughout most of my life that being able to read my handwriting is an acquired art and skill), I may choose to type out my road map after I initially write it out. This provides a time to be a little flexible and be honest with how you learn and commit things to memory best. This allows you to go into the next day with a plan and a dedicated mind-set. Through creating your road map, you will move from motivation to dedication through consistency. This is beyond key, so go back and highlight it. Write it down. Say it out loud. Again, motivation may get you started, but it is dedication built by being consistent that will carry you further and allow you to reach your goals.

Now back to creating your road map. The question we are asking ourselves as we are creating our steps of action that will make up the road map is "What is necessary to make this happen?"

Ask this question at each step to break out all the small additional steps that will need to be done to get that bigger step accomplished. Let's say we have a goal around finding a job that allows us the freedom to make our own schedule and work from home at least 40 percent of the time with no weekend hours. We start our road map and land on a step about sending out our résumé to the identified employers. If we ask ourselves the magic question of "What is necessary to make this happen?" we will come up with additional steps beyond just planning to send out our résumé. These steps may include locating the current résumé we may have (or creating one if we do not have one), revising the current résumé, identifying how the employers would like the résumé to be submitted, and ensuring we have the résumé ready in the form required (paper, electronic, etc.). This will allow us to be more planful when it comes time to take action. Once we have gone through asking this first question of "What is necessary to make this happen?" and we feel that we have a pretty thorough outline of a road map, we can go back and put it to the test with a few more helpful questions. The next two questions are "Why will this be difficult?" and "Who can help [support, encourage, etc.] me with this?"

These two questions can go hand in hand, and oftentimes we go between the two as we revise and evaluate our road map. As I mentioned before, I will highlight some common barriers you may come up against a little later, which I hope will aid you in planning for how you will handle the answer to the question "Why will this be difficult?" This can lead you to the question "Who can help/support me with this?" and allow us to answer it more specifically and honestly. At times, we also may need to ask ourselves "Why will this be hard?" when it comes to asking a certain person for help. We can tackle that under the barriers section too. If we use the résumé example, perhaps it has been a while since you have looked at a résumé, so you decide that it will be hard because you are not sure what employers are currently expecting or how to represent your current experience in a way that will make you stand out among other candidates. So who can help you? Perhaps your uncle that works in human resources or your neighbor that does interviews for the program she oversees at the nonprofit she works at would be willing.

We need to continue to utilize our creative thinking when thinking about the strengths those around us have. Let's say we cannot think of any person that has the specific skill set or strength we are trying to call upon. It is always helpful to have a go-to list of people we can ask, "Do you know anything about [skill, strength, or knowledge base] or know anyone who does?" Never, ever underestimate the power of networking. This is another key point, so go ahead and grab the highlighter again. Most often, we will need to expand out of our current network of support to get to where we want to go, so get prepared for that.

Take some time now to start your road map. I have provided space for you to first rewrite and visualize your *what* and *why* so they will be easily accessible. For your initial attempt at starting at the finish line you want to cross, work toward the starting line while asking, "What is necessary to make this happen?" Once you have completed the first draft, you can move on to utilize the next space with the prompt of "Why will this be hard?" You can make notes for each step from the first draft of both the answer to the question and the possible solutions you will use to overcome the identified barrier. The next space gives you an opportunity to go deeper into the solution-seeking by focusing on the question "Who can help me with this?" for each step from the second draft. This will allow you to identify supports for the initial steps of the road map and for the potential barriers you identified. The last space will allow you to create a new draft with all of the data you gathered in your assessment to create a plan you will be able to utilize in taking action!

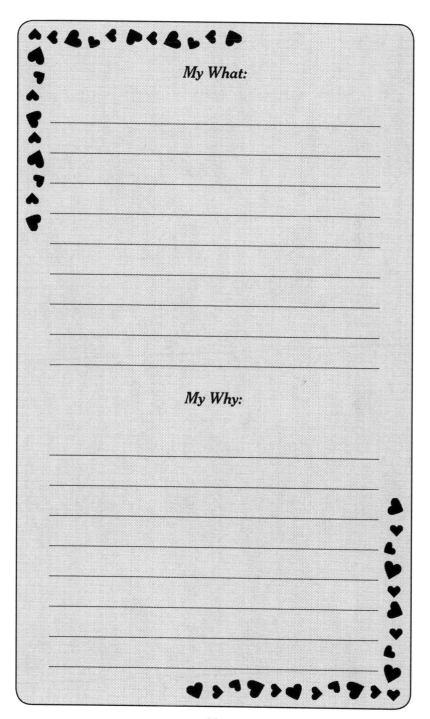

My What:

_____

_____

_____

_____

_____

_____

_____

My Why:

_____

_____

_____

_____

_____

_____

_____

My Road Map:
What is necessary to make this happen?

My Road Map:
Why will this be difficult?

My Road Map:
Who can help me with this?

_____
_____
_____
_____
_____
_____
_____
_____
_____
_____
_____
_____
_____
_____
_____
_____
_____

My Road Map:

_____
_____
_____
_____
_____
_____
_____
_____
_____
_____
_____
_____
_____
_____
_____
_____
_____
_____
_____

The Barriers to Success and Happiness

So you have taken the time to develop your road map and to ask all three magic questions to break out each step. Awesome! Take a moment to celebrate this success. Reward yourself with something you love. It can be helpful to identify what this reward will be ahead of time so you have something to work toward in the planning process. It is equally helpful to do the same along the way while carrying out the steps on your road map. Obviously the biggest reward will be accomplishing the big goal, but it is so important to find ways to celebrate the same successes along the journey. Our brains love a good contingency plan, meaning that if we do A, we get B or we will avoid C. For example, many people do not follow the posted speed limit all of the time. I am not pointing any fingers or placing blame; I am just stating a truth I think most people can agree with. So as a person is speeding down the roadway and spots a police officer, he or she will hit the brake pedal to avoid a ticket and fine. If I slow down, then I won't get a ticket and have to pay money that I would rather spend on some new shoes. Another example most people can agree on is that most people would stop showing up to work if they stopped getting paid.

Most people find the motivation to show up to their place of employment because of the promise of payment for the work they do. We can use this to our advantage along our goal-accomplishing journey. Building in small little incentives will help us stay the course. Making a list of all the things you love and enjoy can be helpful. As we move deeper into the last part of the planning phase, we can use the items on the list to help pump us up to get to the next checkpoint. The final step is scheduling time to take the steps. As we step up to the starting line with our map of the course we have outlined, we need to plan out when and how we will take these steps. Grab your day planner, a calendar, notebook, phone, etc. Just as writing down our goal and the steps into a road map increases our chances of achieving them, scheduling in the specific times when you will do them goes hand in hand. If we just say, "I will get to it when it is convenient or as I find the time," we waste all the planning and preparation we have done. We will find the time to make this convenient only if we decide that it is a priority and schedule the steps into our daily routine. This means having to change up when you do specific things, or finding ways to be more efficient in the tasks that will have to stay on your to-do list. The biggest excuse that trips people up is the idea that there is no time. There is always time for the things in our lives that we view as necessary and important. We have to start viewing the steps to this goal as things on the top of that list. Take your road map out and make a note of how much it will take to complete each step individually. This will help in the planning process.

If you have decided to push on, awesome! I know this is not easy, but I can promise it will be worth it. Let's get back to the schedule. When you are looking at where to schedule in each step, you need to be realistic about how much time it will take. I recommend giving yourself more time than you think it will take; that way you do not leave a step uncompleted or unstarted because of the time constraint you created in the scheduling of the step. Additionally, it will keep you from rushing through and not getting the maximum benefit from the step you outlined. This also creates an opportunity for extra time if you finish before the allotted time scheduled. Bonus! Also, when you are scheduling, pay attention to what else is on the agenda for that day. If you have a step that will be particularly stressful, you probably do not want to schedule that right before an important meeting with your child's school. If a step requires you to travel to one part of town and you have to be back on the other side of town for the next meeting, that might not work out so great. Also be mindful if your step involves someone else; you will need to be mindful in order to make your schedule work with theirs. If we decide to call someone to ask him or her a question as one of our steps, that does not mean that person will answer, so we will need to be proactive in planning out the time needed to complete steps involving our amazing supports and networking partners.

As I mentioned before, when you are scheduling steps, be sure to plan in rewards for yourself. If you have to travel to the other side of town and your favorite coffee place is near there, plan to stop on the way back to celebrate accomplishing the goal. Pull out the list and see which activities can be paired with which steps to give you the biggest bang for your buck (and time). Just be sure to allow time in your schedule for it! Nothing is more disappointing than missing a planned opportunity to do something nice for yourself. I would also like to note that if a planned step is not taken at the scheduled time for whatever reason (traffic, childcare falling through at the last second, the dog vomiting all over the kitchen as you were out walking, a natural disaster, etc.), the step needs to be rescheduled immediately. The moment you realize you will not be able to complete the step as planned, take sixty seconds to review your schedule and reschedule that step and any subsequent steps as necessary to stay on track.

The less rescheduling we have to do, the better, obviously, but I get that life happens. If we are getting in the habit of following the schedule we are creating and getting efficient at this type of planning, we will start to create small pockets of free time that we can use to make up for lost time due to crises or emergencies that might arise. This is one of the reasons that the visual schedule is so important. So if you have been reading this section and thinking that you do not currently have a way of keeping track of your life, then get on it immediately! Again, go with what works for you. I tried to go electronic a few years back, but I continue to have more success with an actual handheld day planner. I will say that no matter what medium you decide to go with, it should be something that is easily accessible throughout the day and something with which you can track everything you have to complete daily, weekly, and monthly. If you decide that you are going to use an app or calendar on your phone and you cannot have access to your phone at work, this can be problematic. In the same way, your desk calendar will prove to be cumbersome to carry around, which will result in you not doing so. We want to be able to access, review, and evaluate our daily and weekly plans easily. This will allow for more planned steps to be completed, less double-scheduling, and less frequent rescheduling of steps. This ultimately means more opportunities to move yourself forward and increase your joy in life!

Evaluating the Plan
for Barriers

Are you ready to rock? On your mark, get set, go! It may seem obvious that we now need to travel through the road map, yet this is the place so many people get stuck. They take so much time getting ready to be ready to make a change. While having a plan is essential, do not get stuck in the planning phase. We do not have to have all the answers to get started. As long as we have outlined our road map, we have what we need. As we move through the steps, we will follow a simple assessment process to keep us moving forward and to fill in the details regarding what specific steps may be necessary to continue on our road map toward our goal. When we take one of the steps on the road map, we can ask ourselves questions such as "Where did this get me?" "What did I learn?" "How did this go?" and "What worked, and what did not?" This will allow us to learn what good stuff we can take with us, as well as whether or not the step we took was completed. If the step fell short of where we thought it would get us, that will lead us to gather a new assessment from taking the step, and we can develop our next steps from this new information. We can reprioritize where to go next and plan to take the next steps. And remember: then we take the action as planned!

This will bring us back to evaluate what we learned and what successes we can celebrate. This simple process will ensure that we can plan for unseen barriers; it will also support us to be flexible if new opportunities or situations move us to different paths on our road map. Maybe when you were connecting with your old friend who is in publishing about supporting you in learning the process of getting your book published, he or she connected you to an editor that also happens to be a college professor that knows of a need in a department of the university in the field that you work in and offers you the opportunity to hand your résumé to the dean of that department. Your initial goal may have been linked to being a published author, yet this new opportunity has now presented itself to you. We need to be prepared in order not to miss out on situations like this just because we are so focused on our specific goal. By evaluating how the step of connecting with the editor went, you can determine that she will be able to edit your book, and there is then a new opportunity to assess what action steps may need to be taken in light of this new information.

Some people may choose to incorporate this new information into their goal by reframing the goal to include a statement around teaching or connecting with this specific population through being a published author and professor, or by having their goal be about changing careers to be able to earn a living through having a positive influence on others in the community, while others may choose to create a separate goal—especially if there is not a direct link between the book and teaching in an university setting. Let's also not forget that we also have the option to pass up opportunities. If you are not excited about an opportunity, then maybe you should file this away as a "Thank you, but not right now" situation.

Let's discuss those barriers in more detail—both the ones we anticipate and those that come out of left field as we are going along through our road map. One of the best ways to have the barriers already identified and planned for is to really visualize and walk through the whole process of the step you are getting ready to take. Also, I want to again highlight the importance of being honest with ourselves when we are asking those key questions so we are not relying on willpower as the answer for most of those barriers.

If we are focusing on the goal of being healthier and we are taking the step of adding in exercise four times a week for at least thirty minutes a day, we had better take some time to challenge ourselves when the plan is "I will just get up at 5:45 a.m." If you are not currently in the habit of waking up at this time, chances are you will find this difficult. This does not mean that you are not strong or motivated; you just are not used to it. You will want to consider whether or not you are someone that needs to hit the snooze button in order to set your alarm accordingly. Based on this new time, we can consider what time we should go to bed to ensure we are well rested. Another thing we can consider to make the morning smoother is choosing what we will wear for our workout and getting those items laid out the night before. Heck, I have friends that sleep in their workout clothes to get in an extra two minutes of sleep and have one less thing to think about in the morning when it is cold, and perhaps dark. As you do this, you can visualize the workout you will do to set your mind in the right direction of already feeling as though we accomplished it and can do it. I have found this especially helpful on days when I have to work out in my basement to utilize the heavier weights rather than the toy room on our first floor, which is typically the space I use. Remember that it takes time to build a habit, and the best way to do that is to be consistent in your actions. The best way to build consistency is by planning and setting ourselves up for success. Here's a fun little story about my journey into fitness to highlight not only the importance of identifying the barriers to be able to plan for them but also the ability we have to accomplish what we want when we do this repeatedly over time.

I grew up being surrounded by sports and physical activity all my life. My parents coached, and my sister and I played almost every sport that you can think of. Because fitness and exercise were part of my everyday life, I never really thought much about it as far as questioning whether or not I enjoyed it or wanted to enjoy it. I just did it because that was what I did to continue to become a better athlete. This continued into college, where I stopped playing organized sports, and the university did the most unforgivable thing and built a brand-new state-of-the-art gym at the top of the biggest hill on campus. At least that was the running joke for all of us that lacked the motivation and desire to have it be a building we frequented. We can conclude this by saying that I was less than dedicated to including fitness in my life on a daily basis.

I continued in this pattern until my late twenties, when I did something that I had sworn I never would. I should go ahead and acknowledge that scenarios such as this led to my life-changing and mind-opening events. I joined a gym. Now, this did not come from a place of wanting to focus on my health and wellness and be the best version of me. That point comes way later in the story. Not to ruin it for you, but those reasons are the cognitions that I use to continue and to stay consistent. If you are wondering why this was something I had always said I would not do, it has to do with the idea of continually paying money to access a place I had little desire to be in, since most of the gyms in my area were known more for their social aspect than the exercise component, as well as the idea of working out in public on machines that other people sweat and do who knows what else on. I apologize to anyone who is reading this with a goal to go to the gym more often if this cognition was less than helpful. Let's see if I can save you by explaining how I got over that cognition for myself.

For starters, I have a neighbor that has a heart bigger than the world. He is so kind and passionate that when he asks others to do something, they just do it. He also happens to be a SPIN® instructor. So when he told me that he wanted me to take one of his classes on a Wednesday night, there was no real way to say no. Then he continued to pull into my driveway every Wednesday night after that. If you have ever taken a SPIN class, you know the adjustment period needed to get comfortable with the seat. For me it took about three classes to be able to stop hurting in places I have never hurt before and really be able to see the benefits to this whole SPIN thing. So I joined the gym to be able to take additional classes and have access to a few other amenities. I became a regular and forged some great friendships with the other regulars in the classes I took. This emphasized the idea that exercise is always more fun with a buddy and explained the necessity of supports and community when accomplishing hard things.

I continued working on my fitness through my pregnancy with my daughter. I was physically in the best shape of my life at that point in time. I believe this helped me have a healthy pregnancy, and a quick recovery period after my daughter's delivery. Because of my C-section, I could not return to physical activity for many weeks. This, along with several other stressors—including the lack of sleep and the whole first-time mom thing—led to some difficult experiences with postpartum anxiety. One of the added barriers related to this was that I did not want to leave my daughter to go to the gym, especially when I returned to work. I may not have foreseen this barrier, but I could still overcome it. I began utilizing the equipment in our house to add fitness back into my life. I was not as consistent as I had been prior to her birth, but I was still finding ways to move my body, and I continued to work on my nutrition, which had become a focus and learning point during my pregnancy.

When the decision was made to add another minion to our family, I refocused on my fitness and continued to focus on nutrition. I began to think about what I would need postpartum to try to avoid depression and anxiety as much as possible. This led me to reconnect with an old friend from my earlier years who was doing specific programs that allowed one to work out at home. I joined her and the community this connection led me to. I was always skeptical of having true supports and friends through technology, until some of my biggest supports and educators became people I had never met. It was these people I would check in with at the crack of dawn, when I would get my workout in. Let's remember that I was used to working out in the evening. I always said I was someone that could not work out in the morning. It is more difficult for me to get through the workout when my body is not warm from movement throughout the day. Yet now with two children, there were more barriers to plan for in the evening, so I became a morning warrior. I would also like to emphasize that my son was amazingly good at so many things, but sleep was not one of them. So even though I was not getting an exorbitant amount of sleep, I knew I would still have more energy and feel stronger mentally if I got up to get my workout in. I am also still aware that it is physically easier for me to do certain forms of exercise, such as cardio, later in the day, yet I still have my daily alarm set for that early-morning wake-up call.

As I am writing this book, my son is just over three years old, and I can say that fitness is an essential part of my life and daily routine. I am by no means an exercise or nutrition guru or expert, yet most people in my life that know me well know my dedication to these things in my life. I never set out to have this be the case; I just wanted to feel better in my own skin and in my mind. This has led to the laying out of workout clothes and equipment the night before, the preparation of meals and snacks ahead of time, and the planning of barriers as new situations arise. I have downloaded and saved workout videos I need for the next morning during storms in case we lose power. I plan out workouts so I can do specific kinds of workouts on vacations, given the space and equipment I will have access to. I do this not to look a certain way but to normalize the need for self-care and self-prioritization to my children, as well as to feel the way I do when I am on track with my fitness and nutrition. It is never about perfection, and as I write this I am getting more dialed in after the holidays, during which I enjoyed my fair share of cookies. For me it is about owning my choices, evaluating where they led me, and planning to continue to move forward. I enjoyed every one of those cookies, and I knew I would indulge over the holidays. Now I am choosing to eat healthier foods that I enjoy to ensure I am feeling my best and staying the healthiest I can. This may require being more mindful when it comes to eating out and avoiding certain foods that are still floating around, yet it is always easier to stick to the steps I have planned out than trying to just say no.

To stick with the fitness theme, willpower is like a muscle. Just like any other muscle, it can start out strong, but over time it fatigues—especially when we use it excessively. The way to get the best results is to train with a plan and utilize programming that will maximize results. This holds true for building your biceps and your abs, as well as for building your goals. The key takeaway here is that we need to be strong in our commitment to our *what* and *why*, and flexible in the road map.

As you evaluated your road map for next steps, did you identify barriers that came from a specific place? Perhaps these barriers originate from within or from a specific person. In the hope of providing you with the best support possible, here is an opportunity to write your newly revised road map, including the evaluation questions. While drafting this, see if you identify any specific kinds of barriers that are more difficult to identify a solution to. In the following chapters, I break out common barriers people face, as well as possible solutions to better support you in your process of planning, implementation, and evaluation.

My Road Map:
Where did this get me? What did I learn? How did this go? What worked, and what did not?

All the Barriers from People

Remember when we discussed change being hard for us? Yeah, so that applies to every person. When you finally decide that you are done living in your current version of difficulty and you start making positive changes in the ways you think and act, other people will not always be ready to be your biggest cheerleaders. This applies to any change, no matter how big or small. Sure, there may be a select few that cheer you on. We will come back to these people later, so memorize their names, write them down, and ingrain their faces in your brain. We will need them! For now, let's focus on the people not openly cheering you on. Now, before we start building resentment toward all of our loved ones that are not standing up with pom-poms and chanting positive affirmations for us, let's review why that may be. When we form relationships with people, whether we do so through family, friends, professional situations, romantic situations, etc., we form patterns of behavior with them from the start. This is kind of like a secret handshake. It's a ritual you usually do not even have to think about, and it evolves and builds over time with the people that continue to exist in our lives. Think about it; we all have that friend that is in charge of making plans. We don't even think about reaching out to plan a dinner date, because that's his or her job. Typically we won't just reach out and try to organize something. We just sit back and wonder, *What the hell is the problem with him or her? Why hasn't he or she reached out to me? Is it something I did?* Then the person will reach out, and everything will be right in the world. It's just the way the handshake goes. So when you start to push away negativity and strive to be the better you that you deserve and are committed to being, people around you will try to push you back to your old patterns. They do this not because they don't love and care about you, but rather because their subconscious is kicking and saying, "What the hell is going on? We don't do a double fist bump after the low five! We are going to catch a high five to the face if we don't get back to the routine!" It's up to us to stay committed and allow them the time to learn the new handshake that is forming, or choose not to.

Sometimes part of growing is leaving others behind. We cannot force others to change. I mean, it's hard enough to get ourselves to do something different when we are choosing to change, so it's going to be next to impossible to force someone to change in the way and at the speed we want them to against their will. Some people will come around over time, and they can be added to the first list of awesome cheerleaders. Some people can remain in our lives to serve other purposes, and we will just not include them in the area we are growing in. This may mean less time spent together, or it may just mean filtering what we choose to focus on when we are together. As long as that works for both people, the relationship can stay on track. Others may have to be left behind if they are not serving to make us better. This is not selfish; it's self-protection and self-love. We usually are taught that putting our own needs before anyone else's is selfish. Yet we know that the best way to take care of others to the best of our ability is to take care of ourselves first so we have the mental, emotional, and physical strength to conquer all the things on our to-do list. We all know the plane analogy, in which the flight attendant reminds the passengers that if the oxygen masks drop, passengers should first put on their own before assisting others around them. If you can't breathe, you can't help anyone else. So put on your damn mask, take a deep breath, and let's have these hard conversations to fully prepare you to get after those goals.

Friends

Our actions and beliefs mirror those of the people we spend the most time with. Friendship is the realm where we have the most say, at times, with who these people are. We will need to take a long, hard look at each person we have chosen to have in our lives. We can start by reflecting on where the friendship originated, and then we can look at why we choose to have the relationship continue. Be honest with yourself about what you currently get out of this relationship and how this will support where you are trying to go. I am not going to tell you to start cutting off all your friends or to start viewing them as a means to get something out of them to meet your goal. This is just a true evaluation of the relationships in our lives, how much time and energy we spend on them, and what the payout of that investment is.

This is a healthy way to evaluate all the people in our lives from time to time to see which relationships we want to continue to work on, which ones we want to spend more time in, and which ones we want to move on from. If you reflect on the friendships you have had over the years, you will probably realize that you have done a version of this, and that is why you have developed deeper friendships and gained new friends over time. Other relationships remained the same in all of their greatness, and some people are no longer in your life. During a time when we already feel as if we do not have a ton of time, we will want to be selective in whom we spend time with, as well as with whom we share information about our journey. This may mean a decrease in contact with some people, which may not be met with a ton of positivity from the other person. Just remember that you need to put on your damn mask for you rather than continuing to live your life for others.

In keeping with my transparency, I will add that this may mean some friends will choose to move away from your friendship. We cannot control other people's decisions. This will be especially true for the people you do a lot for when you suddenly have less time to meet their needs. A true friendship is about balance, with both people giving 100 percent; and in times of need, the balance may shift, with one person taking on more for the other person. In a healthy friendship, this is a temporary shift, as in times when we need to take an extra focus on ourselves to rock out a goal, or in times of crisis. If someone cannot get on board with this, the real question becomes, "Was this person a true friend anyway?" This is completely your call. Just keep in mind that your journey toward greatness will be more difficult if you are fighting through a forest of negativity and other people's expectations.

It may be easier to spot the super support friends who are excited for you, offering support, and cheering you on. I love these friends! Give them a high five and a thank-you from me. It may also be easy to spot the joy-suckers who are raining negativity down on your parade. There are some other people in our lives that may be harder to categorize and decide what to do with. Suppose a friend that you hang out with and do fun things together with, such as get your nails done and go out to eat, has a strong opinion on anything that he or she is not currently into. You want to buy a Volvo, and this person drives a Honda, and he or she feels compelled to list all the reasons why his or her car is the best and yours will not be. If your big goal is to be self-employed as a photographer and the other person has a desk job at a company because of the medical benefits, salary, and set nine-to-five schedule, you may want to reconsider sharing your road map and goal unless you are ready to swat away all the negativity that is about to come your way. For the record, this person's opinion has less to do with how he or she feels about you and your choices, and more to do with his or her own insecurities. Because of this, we will leave it at that and just allow this person to sit in his or her own issues. Enjoy the person's company over some delicious pizza while planning your next shopping excursion to carry on the relationship if you want to, and go back to one of your cheerleaders to discuss your goal. Just be careful not to commit so much time that your commitments interfere in your ability to schedule time for the important people and steps you need to rock that week.

Here's another tricky set of friends. Similar to the opinionated group, these friends are fun to be around and can bring joy to our lives. They may even share a "Good for you!" when we mention our goals. Seems good so far, right? Let's look a little deeper at the way they live their lives. They may work dead-end jobs and may have become complacent in their day-to-day lives even though they may have mentioned that they would like something more. You may hear them say things like "It's as good as it is going to get" or "It's good enough." Heck, this might have been us before deciding to jump all in with this book and start doing some goal-setting. We know that there is no motivation or desire to grow in these individuals. They are not seeking out opportunities to better themselves, which is fine for them, so it's not a judgement, but that also means that their actions will mirror this. This will limit our ability to grow with them. When we suggest taking our monthly get-together for takeout on the road to a restaurant so we can network, this will most likely be met with crickets and then followed up with a big "Thanks, but no thanks." These are not negative relationships, yet they are not the positive-growth relationships that we are seeking either. So again, be smart about your time and how you prioritize it with these friends. Maybe the night in can be used as an incentive for completing some of the steps. These people may be some of the most difficult to leave behind if you outgrow them. I am hopeful your friendships can evolve as you do through accomplishing your goal, but this is not always the case.

What happens when we find that we do not have any friends that fall into the category of people that help push us forward? If we take a hard look at some of our friends, we may find that we also have friends that are great role models in that they have achieved success in the area we are setting a goal in. But sometimes these friends do not support us in moving forward. They do not offer the support or resources needed to make the next step happen. What then? The idea of making new friends sounds terrifying, and sometimes impossible, to most people. I have a theory that the older we get, the harder it is to naturally make new friends. When we are two, all we need is a pile of dirt and another kid. Friendship made. As we get older, there may be fewer social situations we are naturally in that lend themselves to connecting with new people, not to mention the unhelpful thoughts about ourselves and others that get in our way when talking to people we don't know. We will spend more time on the self-defeating cognitions later. What's the solution to meeting new people? Look at every interaction with another person as an opportunity to connect and step outside of your comfort zone.

It is not that we have fewer opportunities to socialize when we are older; it is that we choose not to see them as opportunities, or we find ways to avoid them. We wait in the car to pick up our children at school, or we have our groceries delivered to our house, or we order our coffee through an app and have to run inside the coffee shop with our head down to grab our order and hide back in our car. I am not saying you should spend all of your time talking to every single person, or that you should not utilize technology or other supports to streamline your life and make time for other essential things; but when we are in the place of trying to broaden our network of supports, we have to challenge the idea that there are no people to meet and no places to go to try to meet them. You may have to seek out people within your field yourself to find the connections and resources that will help you advance. You may have to join groups or hire a coach or a therapist, depending on the goal and the barriers. You can even start by just saying something kind to a person in front of you in a line, or to another parent at school pickup. Just stop putting your head down and ignoring the fact that we are surrounded by other people. Start seeking out *your* people—people that will not only encourage and support you but will also hold you accountable and push you to grow. These are your people. I hope you already have at least one person that falls into that category. It's up to you to go out and find others that are searching for you on their journeys. Link arms and go out and conquer the world.

Family

Our families are some of the people that know us the best, yet it does not always feel like that. We would all like to believe that our family members will back us no matter what, which is why it is sometimes even more disappointing when they don't, or when they make comments that feel less then supportive. For now, let's put our spouse, partner, or significant other and any children to the side. They can have their own section.

We are picking on our parents, grandparents (and any other generations that may be still around to share their opinions), siblings, aunts, uncles, and cousins. These are all the people that may be in our lives that we have some genetic or legal connection to (or they may be related to us by marriage when they choose to become legally obligated to someone we have a genetic connection to). Oftentimes we are taught to respect these people simply because of their relation to us. This respect is sometimes linked directly to "listening" or "obeying" what these people say. We often make choices in our adult lives because of what our parents or "Auntie Mildred" will think. We may still be making life choices because we want to please or appease certain family members. This can hold us back in so many ways.

If we are not aware of our making choices to please family, we continue to repeat the patterns of behavior from our childhood into our adult life when we are with our family, even when we have moved beyond this behavior with others. Ever walk into your parents' house and notice that when you go to sit down at the table for dinner, everyone sits in the same seats they sat in back when you were seven? There was a time when my mom and I disagreed about something, and she was starting down the path of statements that usually led to me being grounded or sent to my room. I was probably crying, because that's what I always did when I was in trouble. The difference that made both of us pause was when I stopped crying and said, "I have a question." I pointed to an envelope on the kitchen table and asked if she should pay the mortgage since she was grounding me in my own home—because this all happened in the kitchen of the house I lived in when I was in my twenties. It was a sassy and uncharacteristic statement for me to have made, but it makes for a great story now. I am a sassy and—I like to think—witty person in my adult personal life, so why not be so in my life with my family?

Why can't the "follow the rules and don't talk back" young person be this version of herself as an adult? Luckily for me, my mom also experienced a similar morphing of personality through her life, so she welcomes these traits in me. It was not easy initially, since this was outside of the dance we always did. We can laugh about it now, and we still refer to times when I became more assertive, such as when I told my mom "it's none of your business" when she asked about the details of a trip I had taken to the Bahamas. There were not a lot of happy faces when it actually happened, but it is super comical over a decade later.

The point is that we get to choose who we want to be with every person we encounter, including our family. If we approach this from a kind and respectful place, hopefully everyone will get on board over time. If you can encourage your family to see how your goal is bettering your life and making you happy, this should allow them to get on board more quickly. Just be prepared to stay the course if they are not jumping on board right away. You can spend some time hearing their concerns about the changes and choices you are making in your efforts toward your goal to try to find the potential for positive reframing within them. For example, I had several relatives that were concerned about my home birth and the potential for an emergency that would require medical intervention beyond what was available in my house. Instead of hearing the comments as negative possibilities or doubts about my goal, I would reframe this as them stating their concern from a place of love. I chose to see this as their way of stating how much they cared about the well-being of me and my baby. I focused on the shared outcome of a healthy and happy delivery. This allowed me to feel more positive toward my relationship with them and our time spent together. Then I could spend additional time with other people, talking about how awesome this was all going to be. So if all or some of the members of your family are not joining your fan club, choose to surround yourself with other people that are cheering you on, and be smart about what information you choose to share. If your desired outcome is to get support or to change their minds, and you know that is unlikely, perhaps you should refrain from sharing your excitement for now so their opinions do not remain a barrier to your happiness.

Coworkers and Work Friends

Our work friends are a great support to make it through the workday and beyond. They understand the special kind of stress and aggravation that your job may add to your life. I don't say that to say that your job sucks and you should quit, or anything along those lines. I hope you love your job, or at least some aspect of it. Yet even if we love what we do, there will be moments or aspects of our work that feel just like that—work. So it's great to have people to vent to that truly understand what you are going through. There is nothing more frustrating than already being stressed about something specific at work and having to explain that thing to someone else just to be able to vent about it. That is not a great use of time; nor is it productive. At one point in my career within the agency-based work I did, I oversaw a program that provided treatment for adolescents that displayed problematic sexual behaviors. My staff and I heard and saw some pretty explicit things over the years. Let's just say the details are not something the common person in society wants to hear about. Typical responses I would receive from well-meaning supports would range from "You're so amazing for the work that you do; I could never do it" to "I don't know why you want to work with those people." Neither response is particularly helpful when all I wanted to do was unload about how hard the day was so I could regroup to take on the next day.

Of course, such comments came up only if I could get as far as to mention what was stressing me out. Most people would be so horrified by words like "anal penetration" and "masturbation" that the conversation would end before it really started. I totally get it. So without my work friends who also got it, I would have been lost.

If you are lucky enough to have these great people in your life, and you decide that you want to set and work toward a goal that would move you beyond where you are at work, whether that be through a promotion or through moving on to something else, you may find that these great supports are not so great anymore. There can be many things at play here. Maybe you are so amazing at what you do, or you are such a great support to them, that they do not want to lose you. Maybe they feel the same way but have not made the leap to set the goal and this makes them feel a certain kind of way about you. Maybe they feel you are judging their choice of job since they are still doing the work and you no longer desire it. Whatever their hang-up about your desire for something different for yourself, remember: it's their issue. Let them feel how they feel and think what they think.

You will need to find ways to remind yourself that it is your life and that you deserve to live it out in the way that will bring you the most joy. You cannot make work-related decisions based solely on the thoughts and feelings of your coworkers, boss, staff, or people you may serve through your work. Set your goals to bring out the best in you for you and your current situation. This was one of the pieces that kept me in my agency-based work for so long. I did truly enjoy being around the majority of the people I worked for and with. I loved being a part of someone's professional growth and building relationships with people. It was them that I pictured in my mind when I started visualizing new goals, and I would hold on to their images to get me to show up the next day. I will be honest; this can go on only for so long.

I had to admit to myself that this approach was causing me to burn out, and that meant I was not going to be effective in my role the way I wanted to. It was also bleeding over into my personal life. I had to change my focus back to me and what would make me truly happy. You may have to look beyond your work friends for this support, and that can be okay. You can also carry your work friends beyond just your job. Just make sure you are starting with what will fill your cup with joy; then decide who those people are to get you there. This can be a great opportunity to network with people within your field of choice to seek out their guidance, support, and skills to further your knowledge base and add to the opportunities immediately in front of you. You never know where a conversation can lead, or who knows who.

Make a list of questions you may have about where you are trying to head with your work, then begin to identify whom you can ask those questions to. Be open to where this path leads you, because it is rarely a straight line. Be excited about the many points you will travel to through these connections, which will create a beautiful picture once you connect the dots.

Spouse or Partner

Most of us would like to think that our partners in crime or spouses (or whatever else we would like to term the person we are in a committed relationship with) would be our biggest supporters—especially when we are looking to make positive changes in our life. For those of you for whom this is true, my heart is so happy it could explode. For those of you that have been waiting to get to this section because your significant other is less than thrilled with the goal that you are setting and working toward, I am here for you. We can take a moment to have our pity party about how much it sucks that our partner isn't supporting our efforts to kick ass with A, B, and C. When we have spent enough time acknowledging the injustice of it all, let's regroup to problem-solve. There are a couple of things we will want to assess.

Did we discuss this goal and our plan prior to taking steps and, because of this, start to make changes that could be impacting this other person as well? Sometimes we get so excited about our goal that we just jump right into our action steps. If we are cohabitating with someone else, this usually means that our plan will have an impact on that person in some way. If you decide that you want to eat healthier and you throw out all the junk food in your house, including your spouse's favorite after-dinner snack, chances are your spouse will be grumpy with you when he or she opens the cabinet that night. I am a food lover, so don't mess with my food, especially without my consent. It's always a good idea to clue the other person in to the changes you are looking to make. Is the reason that you didn't tell the person in the first place not an oversight, but rather intentional because you are afraid of his or her reaction? We may need to spend some time problem-solving this one to set us up for success. This is one of the specific cognitions I tackle later in the book, so make a note!

When I told Mike I was leaving the agency, he asked questions. Of course they were questions about things I was already concerned about, such as how much money I could make at my private practice, how much medical insurance would cost, etc. How dare he ask the questions that would make the most sense to ask, since they directly impacted him and our kids! To be clear, he just asked the questions because he didn't know the answers, as I handled all the finances for the house. He never used a tone that implied he was telling me I shouldn't leave. I am fairly confident he was just as ready for me to leave so I wouldn't be stressed and crying all the time.

Yet, because I was still concerned with these issues, and didn't have concrete answers for his questions, I got defensive. I am sure you would not be surprised if I told you that this never leads down a great path for communication. What I really wanted was for him to say, "Hooray let's quit tomorrow!" I missed that his questions were his way of saying, "Let's do it! Let's plan to make it happen." Once I took a step back and verbalized where I was getting stuck, I was able to hear where he was coming from. This allowed him to support me in the way I needed, and for us to work together—heck, motivate the crap out of each other—to move forward. It never hurts to check in to make sure we have it right, and to voice what we need. We need to find a way to get on the same page.

Some of what was discussed previously in the family section applies here too. Perhaps we need to allow our partner to feel how he or she feels even if we differ. Mike may never join me for a 5:30 a.m. workout, but that can be fine. I've expressed my need for him to not comment on how early and dark it may be so I can go about doing what I need to do to take care of me. But let's say it's something more serious. I am sure many people are reading this and thinking of their goal that will change their life, and their partner has responded with a big "That's not happening!" The goal could be a dream job that would require a big move, having kids, or investing in a best friend's restaurant. What then? What do we do when the thing we want most seems out of reach because of our partner? We need to bring in some big reinforcements for this one.

By this I mean we need to spend some serious time assessing how important this goal is to us, and the *why* around it. We can present this to our partner, and ask him or her to explain why he or she is opposed. This is a great process to work out in therapy with a trained "referee" to ensure you and your partner are playing by the rules. Here are some rules I have utilized in working through this process, which I encourage you to use should you not have the ability to hire a professional. The first rule is to discuss only one person's perspective at a time, and when responding, do so only to validate what the other person is saying or to reflect on something we heard him or her say. It is about hearing the other person, not arguing or proving why we are right. Once we have gained insight into each other's perspective, we can develop a list of pros and cons to both options. In the example of the big move, we would create a list of the benefits and the downsides to moving, as well as the benefits and downsides to not moving. We do not want to compare the two options to each other, because we will miss some of the key points we will want to consider.

Once we have compiled each of the four lists, we can rank the items listed. This can be done together or done separately and then reviewed together. We will want to pay attention to where items fall in prioritization for each person, and then we can discuss where this leaves us. This should be helpful in opening up the lines of communication and allowing us to be on the same page in pursuing the initial goal. Sometimes the goal may need to be tweaked after a compromise was made. To go back to the moving example, maybe the spouse isn't willing to relocate because he gives his own job higher priority and needs to be close to his mother for the next year because of her failing health, yet he would be on board a year from now. The couple could then use the same process to weigh the pros and cons of one person moving first and the other joining after a year, or both waiting. Another example would be a situation in which the spouse will not move but will help in a more local job search to support the person in finding a comparable dream job, and if that is not possible, they will reopen the conversation.

Ultimately, if a partner or spouse does not want to get on board and this is a goal that impacts the lives of both people in the relationship, the same process may be used to weigh the pros and cons of going for the goal, as well as those of ending the relationship. Both of these are separate evaluations and should not be taken lightly. I am not trying to break up families, and I am definitely not telling anyone to walk away just because things got hard or someone didn't get his or her own way. This piece is a last resort, and you are the only person to know when the time has come to take a look at it.

In using this method you should be able to decide which road is the way to go next on your journey, and it should give you a result you can feel content in. Neither choice is an easy one, yet the things that matter the most rarely are. If you put in the hard work to reach that final decision, you will be able to move forward knowing you did everything you could to make yourself and your partner happy, even if it doesn't play out the way you thought it would. At least it will be a choice made by you, for you, and not just because someone said no.

Just as it is essential to the growth process to evaluate our road map, it is equally essential to evaluate the relationships that we have in our life. The same questions from our continual evaluation of our road map can be applied to our relationships. Knowing how those around us are adding value to or subtracting value from our lives allows us to proactively take steps to strengthen and foster those relationships that add value, as well as create space regarding the ones that inhibit growth and joy.

All the Barriers from Within

This takes us to the next set of barriers—ourselves. Where do we even begin with this one? There has been an underlying tone alluding to this from the beginning. We are the ones that make the choice to listen to the feedback from our friends and family and make decisions based on it. Our friends and family do not make us feel or believe anything. It is our own thoughts on their opinions that draw out our emotional responses. We are also now aware that we can choose how to respond, both physically and emotionally, to these opinions.

So let's dig in to the self-talk and internal dialogue that occur all day long within our own heads. I am being purposefully redundant here to emphasize that this is about *ourselves*.

We need to spend some time listening to how we talk to ourselves. You are probably aware of the idea that our brains are programmed, both by nature and nurture, to focus on the negative. It may be that our brain does recognize differences from an early age. It is not until later that we are taught in some way that different equals negative. This is when we start to trip ourselves up. We notice that people have differences from us, and that other situations or experiences are different from our own. We then come to view such differences as negative and inadequate. We need to start by challenging this thought that different is negative. Different is just different. The blue fish is just a blue fish, and a red fish is just a red fish. One does not have to be better than the other. Now let's challenge the outlook on negativity, which does not have to be the deep, dark hole we make it out to be. It can be seen as a challenge or barrier, yet it creates an opportunity to grow and learn. Without these learning and growing opportunities, we would never truly have something to celebrate. I like to compare this to giving birth. For all you mothers out there, regardless of how the baby enters the world, it is painful and challenging both mentally and physically. Yet this is the story of how your child entered the world and you met for the first time. Hopefully this makes your list of best days ever! We work though the hard part to get to the end result, which is an amazing payout! For those of you that may not connect with the above comparison, think of a really difficult assignment you completed in school—one you spent a lot of time working on. How great did you feel when you received a good grade on it? So push yourself to start to redefine "negative," and include these places for growth and learning into your definition of life and yourself through your internal strength.

Finding Your Strengths

I love asking people to make a list of their strengths and the things they like about themselves. It is one of the fastest ways to assess how much work we have ahead of us. Sadly, most people's lists are short. This may be because they truly do not have anything to add to the list, or because they have been taught that identifying good qualities within us is boastful or can be seen as bragging. Many times people do not put items on the list because other people are better at certain things than they are, so they do not identify those things as strengths. If you are not going to win an award or have not received an Olympic gold medal for something you have done, that does not mean it is not a strength you possess.

The key is just focusing on you, not by comparison of anyone else, and certainly not based on what others have told you. We do that often also. We decide whether something is a strength or a quality someone likes about us based on opinions and feedback from others. It can still feel great when someone compliments you on something, but the starting point should be how you feel about it. Whether it is your organizational skills, crafting ability, willingness to volunteer, or ability to plan an event, start by asking yourself whether you enjoy it and whether it is something that brings out the best in you. We need to let other people feel the way they feel and think what they think. That's their business, so get your nose out of it. It's their job to worry about what's going on for them. We have enough on our plates as it is, so stop trying to do other people's jobs. Just as it is at our actual places of employment, when we do someone else's job, we do not receive his or her paycheck in addition to our own. We just do double the work for the same pay. This is the same thing. Just stick to your job, which is identifying what makes you the amazing version of you that you are today. Let's take some time to identify the strengths we possess. Make sure to really break each quality out, since many may be intertwined in one. For example, if you identify that you are a great parent, follow up by identifying what specifically you do that makes you a great parent. This will create several more qualities on your list. Flip to the end of the chapter to start your list!

Be You

Being able to identify what speaks most to you also applies when deciding what kind of goal to set. It is great to surround yourself with people who inspire you and have achieved successes you idolize. Yet we have to be cautious not to try to become these people. You are your own unique self, and you need to lead your own unique life. Do not set out to become someone else that already exists; nor should you try to follow all the specific steps that person's road map took him or her on to achieve his or her goals. Your process will be unique based on what you have already experienced, your own set of strengths, and the efforts you put into your journey. No two people can live out exactly the same life, so let's not bother trying. We need not compare ourselves to others; nor should we try to be them. We can simply be inspired to know that anything is possible if we just try and believe in our ability to achieve what we decide to achieve.

There will be times when this becomes more and more difficult to do. There is a limit to what I can cover in this book regarding working past current thought patterns due to past experiences. I want to start by acknowledging how difficult that process of letting go of the past can be. As a therapist, I have had the honor to walk with many people down this very difficult, challenging path. This has also allowed me to have the repeated experience of watching people utilize their internal strength to rise above this. I have witnessed so many people that have made the decision to not be defined by their past, and start to make a new future in themselves. So I feel it is my responsibility to believe it is possible for every single person on this planet to do the same. This is why I want to pay this forward, and I hope that you will believe that this holds true for you as well. When there are times during which you need that additional support, there is nothing more worth celebrating than asking for the support you need. Whether you ask a trusted friend, a family member, or a professional, it is essential that you surround yourself with the people that will help you through this process as you work through difficult memories, situations, and thought patterns. You are not weak because you needed to ask for help; you are strong because you found the courage to do so, thereby holding yourself accountable to stay in an uncomfortable place in order to come out victorious on the other side. This is never easy, yet I promise it will be worth it. You just need to stay the course.

Staying Committed

This takes me to the next place we get stuck in our own heads. When I say that we need to stay the course, I mean we need to continue to stay committed no matter how long it takes. I have seen people deem their attempts a failure after trying for only a short time. When we develop our road map, we might have a general idea of how long something might take. We also need to be patient and flexible enough to stick with the road map when our action steps have not gotten us quite to where we were trying to go. If we took the initial steps we created but we did not achieve our goal in the timeline we created in our head, that does not mean that we failed. We fail only if we quit on ourselves and toss the goal away.

When I shared my story of setting the goal of being my own boss to ensure I had the flexibility to be present for myself and my family, there was an underlying message that the original goal was missing the part about being my own boss. When I was first introduced to private practice, I joined a friend's practice, taking on a few clients on the side to make extra money, since my focus was solely on paying my bills and growing professionally. After my daughter's birth, I was focused only on having enough income to support my family and having a flexible schedule that would allow me to spend enough time with her. The first idea was private practice because I did not see how it would be possible to have these things in the current position I held at the agency. I realized I could make more money through my own practice, so I figured out what I needed to have in place to make it a reality. I asked questions, and I was offered incredible support from both sides of my family. Because I was still focused only on the money and the flexibility, it was so easy for me to accept a different position at the agency that required fewer hours when it was presented to me. I could still build my practice as a backup, and I could bring in revenue by bringing others on under my practice. This seemed like a win-win.

As the years progressed, I desired more ability for a flexibility that would allow me to be more present for myself and family, as well as able to work under my own guiding principles and mission statement. Eventually I added on the desire to be my own boss. I share this story to illustrate that I have been working on this same goal for about a decade. The goal may have morphed over time, which I accredit to my ability to assess where each step on my road map took me. It would have been easy to quit along the way, yet I held my *why* tight (both literally and symbolically when we include my kids in this). The process of setting and achieving goals ends only when you stop it. So plan to stay the course, and do whatever is necessary to show up every day. Plan to be committed to achieving something, no matter how long it takes. This is why we celebrate our small victories along the way and set small manageable steps. Do not miss an opportunity to set a goal that seems as if it will take too long. We need to accept that there are no quick fixes and that no amount of time is too long if the outcomes will change our lives for the better.

Another aspect of this to consider is that the goal-setting process is never-ending. Each time you reach a goal, make that your starting line for the next goal. Since who we are is a compilation of all of our experiences up until the present moment, it stands that we continue to grow and evolve every day as we learn and take new steps. As these different, new versions of ourselves, we get to reevaluate where this process has led us and where we want to go next.

For example, whenever I hear that someone has set a goal to lose weight, I hope the process will lead the person not just to a place of losing the desired amount of weight but also to the development of sustainable and generalizable skills that will allow him or her to live a healthy lifestyle he or she enjoys. This includes things like learning about nutrition, exercise, sleep habits, and self-care being incorporated into their daily lives in a positive way. Since one of my most important mantras is "You feel how you feel for a reason," I cannot tell someone what I think his or her goal should be. I also do not try to reframe someone's goal for him or her, because it's not my goal to set. I can support the process, but I do not have to take all the steps and endure the hard times in the process. Each person needs to have these experiences for himself or herself to have the learning opportunities which allow someone to grow into the person he or she will become. The newer version of the person may be the one who can set the bigger goal, which means that the whole process was necessary for this person to be ready to start this new journey. And let's be honest, we appreciate things so much more when we have worked hard for them. Sometimes we need a reminder of this when we just want others to do the work for us. It goes back to the quick fix. If I set the big goal for the person in the weight loss example, it may seem as if we would get to skip the whole first set of steps, which should take less time. This is not how it works, friends.

Each step taken by the person is necessary and is as important as the final results. So remember that when we ask for support, it's about asking for help in doing something, not asking the person to do it for us. The more we take ownership for each step and the plan as a whole, the more likely it is that we will achieve the goal, and the more we will learn and grow. It can be really hard to remember this in the moment, so again, refocus on your *why* and take responsibility for your goals.

Taking Ownership

Another way we get in our own way is by not taking ownership of all our choices. As was just discussed above, it is no one else's responsibility to take our steps for us. Beyond that, it is no one else's fault when we are not making progress with our steps. Sure, there are plenty of barriers, such as people and things that will make our journey more challenging, but if we place the blame on the exterior challenge, we are using it as an excuse to quit. This is a hard mind shift for some people to make. This is also one of the patterns of thinking that will most slow you down and get in the way of you achieving your goals. Say someone wants to open a restaurant and the first person on the list of investors he or she made says, "Thanks, but no thanks." Some people would use this as the reason why they did not open their restaurant. Others would acknowledge that this would not be a reason but would instead be an excuse, and they would continue down the list. Obviously the latter would be more likely to have their ribbon-cutting ceremony.

I am not saying that every situation like this scenario will be so easy to move past. There very well may be barriers that derail us for some time. The point I want you to carry with you is that you hold the power to decide how long you need to be ready to stand back up and continue on, seeing the challenge not as a reason but as an excuse if you let it lead you to giving up. You have the power to choose your perspective of the barriers and challenges. I have been known, at times, as the positive reframe queen. It's raining and you hate the rain? Great, you just saved yourself fifteen minutes blow-drying your hair.

Your place of employment is implementing a new electronic system to track the widgets you make, and you do not love technology? Great, once you push through the learning curve, you will be able to save time at work, which should lower your stress level. You are trying to write your book, and your children keep entering the room you are working in, not to tell you that the house is on fire but to include you in a game of make-believe that clearly is not life-threating? Great, you get the opportunity to practice what you preach. Celebrate the fact that you have created the luxury you wanted—to work from home to get to see their creativity come to life—and kiss them on the forehead as you guide them back to the hundreds of toys they just received from the holidays so you can just finish your work for the time being.

If you give me any crappy situation, I can help you find a way to reframe it so you can see the positive and help you move past the barrier. The part I cannot do is make you think it for yourself and believe it. That is your choice, and only you have the power to decide to see that flip side. Again, I am not telling you which side you have to see; I am telling you that you do have to own that you have the choice, and only you are to blame for the choice you make. No one, including me, can make you feel anything, believe anything, or do anything that you do not want to. You have the choice to decide what you want to think, feel, and believe about yourself and any given situation. One of the best ways to start with this is to focus on taking the emotions out of the decision-making process during the planning phase. It is not that emotions are not important, because they are. This is about acknowledging that we will choose to put our emotions on the back burner to take a clearer look at the facts of any given situation.

When we allow emotions to drive the bus of decision-making, our judgment gets clouded and we veer off course. Instead we can choose to look at the facts to make better-informed decisions. If it is taking me longer than I thought it would to write the book I am working on, I could make excuses about how no one is helping me with childcare.

Maybe I do not want to work on it in front of someone because I think the person will judge me for wanting to write a book, or maybe I do not want to work on it because my daughter wants me to help her with her homework. I can also just own that I have not scheduled in the amount of time necessary this week to achieve my word count goal, so I need to schedule differently to achieve everything that is important.

Evaluate the Emotional Side of Things

Once we have taken ownership, we can more objectively evaluate the emotional side of things. The same process is effective when we are examining how we feel about something, meaning that the more we focus on the positive emotions associated with a situation, the more likely it is that we will move forward with it. This is not to say that we disregard the negative feelings, because they are still part of the equation—and a necessary part at that. Just to be clear, when I am speaking about negative emotions, I am referring to any emotion that will have an adverse effect on the way we want to think, feel, and act. Most often people would think of emotions such as fear, sadness, and anger as negative emotions. To me, it does not actually help to categorize specific emotions such as happiness, excitedness, elatedness, etc. as positive emotions and emotions such as anger, fear, etc. as negative emotions. Each emotion on the whole spectrum of feeling can be essential in the growing and learning process. This is yet another reason why separating out the emotional side of things can be helpful—so we can more effectively examine what emotion is brought out by each step of our road map and each situation. This allows us to know for ourselves whether the emotion we are experiencing is one we want to carry us forward.

For example, I needed my emotions of disgust and anger to push me to make the decision to finally make the leap into full-time self-employment. It was the redirection back to focusing on the positive emotions all those years that kept me in my position. It served me during those times, but when I was ready to make a leap of faith and make a huge change, I needed to focus on different emotions to get me there. I needed to ask myself the questions "How does this emotion serve me? Where is it leaving me, and where can it take me?" Once I was committed to making the leap and I acted on the steps of giving my resignation, I needed to shift gears slightly. I still needed some of that discord to motivate me to get outside of my comfort zone and take the next steps I had outlined for myself that were new for me, and I also needed to add in emotions like excitement to be able to focus on the positive cognitions I wanted to create for myself to believe that I was capable and that I wanted to do things that would be hard and uncomfortable. I share this small piece to highlight the need for and the balance with all of our emotions.

Oftentimes we forget that we need the extremes and the opposite emotions not only for balance but also for the creation of the emotions we typically prefer. There is a duality to everything in life. We can experience hate because we love. We can have sadness because we have joy. We can feel weak and broken in order to have courage and strength. This is why we typically get the angriest, most annoyed, and most upset at the people we love and care about the most, even for what may seem to be small things after the fact. If someone we barely know does not wish us a happy birthday, we may brush it off. If our best friend or significant other forgets our birthday, watch out. It's the love and affective bond we have with someone that will also elicit those strong emotional responses in us.

If you are an animal person, as I am, you may relate to the idea that we add our pets into our lives and families because of the bond and connection we have with them, which is why it is so difficult when they leave us. The benefits of having them in our lives far outweigh the pain of the loss, which is why we choose to focus on each moment we get instead of the inevitable way it will end. To put it bluntly, it hurts at the end because we gave a crap about them during their lives. This example also allows me to highlight the benefits of focusing on each part separately to be able to give ourselves the space to acknowledge that the process of grieving for someone or something that we loved, and learning to live life without that someone or something, is hard and painful. We then get to decide what we can and will do to work with these emotions.

In any situation, there will be a constant balance of understanding how we feel about something and the choice of what we want to do with that emotion. We know that whatever we choose to focus on will multiply, so if we are constantly focused on searching out why we feel a certain way, or when we learn the cause—the thing that is causing the emotion—we will strengthen that emotion. This can be a dangerous cycle, and we can dig ourselves deeper and deeper into a hole that will be more and more difficult to get out of. Instead we can be focused, acknowledging the emotion and focusing on the choices we do have and where those choices can lead us. This is where our power lies.

My Strengths:

All the Barriers from Outside of Us

The world is always so kind as to set up the perfect storm for us when we are finally feeling as though we have a handle on this thing called life. If you have read this far, I am sure you are not surprised by my sarcasm. Sometimes it may feel as if we never leave the storm. I have talked countless people through lists of struggles that have occurred in their lives, and just as many lists have been created about what will happen. This lifetime has not been without tragedy and struggle. It can seem as if no matter where we turn, there is another story of someone suffering from a situation. As someone who copes by learning as much as I can about things I feel uneducated about that matter to me or that have an impact on me, I can appreciate our society's desire for information. This can also lead to a hyper focus on situations that, since we have no control over them, feel overwhelming and hopeless, which in turn creates feelings of fear and hopelessness. It's similar to the notion that we can never fly on an airplane because we believe airplanes crash and malfunction all the time based on stories we see in the media, which are rarely balanced with the statistics of how many flights take off and land without incident.

We have gotten into the habit of believing and holding on to every negative outlier of a situation and creating that as the only truth. We disregard any extreme positives on the other side of the bell curve as unattainable or as not pertaining to ourselves, and we basically ignore the rest of the statistics in the middle, which would represent the most common variable for any situation. I appreciate that it is scary and difficult to push ourselves behind this way of thinking, because that would mean we have hope. It's a small word, but it is scary nonetheless. That is because if we have hope, we then set ourselves up for the possibility of being disappointed or caught off guard, which are things most people do not enjoy.

Yet it is equally uncomfortable to live without hope for long periods of time, and it is not possible to move forward without having at least some hope. We may not be able to change a specific situation we have an issue with, but we can control what aspects we focus on. You may not be able to check the airplane yourself to ensure that it is perfectly functioning, but if you want to take that amazing trip to Tahiti, you can choose to focus on what you can do to get yourself on the plane, and make it through the flight as each moment passes.

A more emotional example would be my experience after Sandy

Hook. As a Connecticut resident and new mom at the time, I became immersed in the story of this tragedy when it occurred. I could not disconnect myself from my desire to listen to the stories through television, the internet and social media. I wanted to hear each person's story to be able to—I think—make sense of what had happened. I was completely unaware of this desire and what felt like a need to be connected to this story until Mike changed the channel of the news story I was watching to check the weather. I was less than calm in my verbal request about changing it back. He calmly asked me if I was all right and if I really thought I needed to watch more about the story. Of course I was defensive at first, and then I was able to see that I did need to take some space. I knew that I could not change what had happened, and I had to let go of my cognitions that I was somehow not being part of the solution by doing the day-to-day things in my own life. I had to focus on the choices I did have. I could be supportive for a good friend that had grown up with a courageous teacher that gave her life to protect her students. I could register to volunteer my time as a therapist for those affected by the events. I could honor, and take extra time to be grateful for, my ability to still hug my daughter and be the best version of me, which she deserved. I sat on my living room floor, talked myself through this, and then took action. I called upon this process when it came time to send my kids to school, especially around the anniversary date. I know that my children will face challenges in their lives, even though I try with all my might to not have that happen. I also have the choice to know that I take an active part in giving them the tools to handle situations that may arise. I choose to focus on the fact that this will give them the best possible chance for success and the gratitude I have for the opportunity to have this struggle in my life. I do appreciate that I get to worry and plan for every little thing that will happen in two additional humans' lives—well, more like three when I include my husband, but I have gotten better at letting a lot of that go, through making the choice of having his life be his. It is not my job to live his life, and it is not his job to live and make decisions in mine. We can play supportive roles, when asked, in each other's lives and situations. It is a choice we all have to focus on the steps of the process so we will find our ability to move to where we want to go.

When we can identify the choices (not that the choice we would most like is actually on the table at any given point in time, but we do, in fact, have some choices in situations), this opens the door for us to decrease unhelpful emotions in frequency, intensity, and duration. One small trick is finding a way to reframe the way we think about external forces. These are events that happen completely outside of us, such as weather, community events, and the actions of other people. These events may have an impact on us, but we are not the driving force behind them. For example, my neighborhood and I had the fun experience of being without electricity for eight days in August after a tropical storm passed through. Everything in our homes runs off electricity, so that meant no lights, hot water, or cooking. It was like camping in our own house, with our amenities taunting us by being within our eyesight yet unusable. Clearly we did not cause the storm; nor did we decide which neighborhoods received services from the electricity provider to repair what needed to be repaired so we could open the refrigerator at will and take a hot shower in our own home. Yet there were repercussions that we had to experience and contend with.

It would have been easy for us to experience this as "This awful situation is happening *to me*." It is true that the situation was happening, yet leaving the last part out allowed me to not fall into being the target or victim of the situation. There was no way for me to avoid this situation, as with many of the situations we face in our lives. I want to emphasize this point. I am not saying we can control the world around us, and in turn, every situation we find ourselves in. I am saying that there are, in fact, situations—horrible and horrific ones at that—that we will find ourselves in. My challenge to you is to end the sentence at "This is happening" and leave off the "to me." This will allow us to start by acknowledging the reality of the situation and the way we feel about it, and it will still allow us to make the jump to being able to identify what choices we have in the situation. When we experience a situation as happening "to" us, it is hard to make the jump to action and to be able to take ownership of the need to do so and the choices we have within. It also gets us in the mind-set that something negative could happen at any time, which will also decrease the likelihood we will take the time to plan and push ourselves to see the choices we have in any given situation. This gets us into a vicious cycle of waiting for problems to arise, which they will. It also leaves us feeling as though we have no control over anything in our lives, and therefore as though we are incapable of bringing about change.

So let's face some hard truths about the world we live in. The world is not out to get any one of us, to the best of my knowledge. It is not helpful to compare our lives, strengths, and struggles to anyone else's. This is rarely helpful, because we are quick to find the reasons why someone is better than we are, which makes us feel as if we are less than they are; and it is also not helpful when we focus on how someone is worse off than we are, as we then feel guilty simply for feeling the way we did about our own struggles. So each one of us will have our own unique circumstances, which include struggles and strengths, and we each have the choice, in every moment, of what we will do with those as our story unfolds. There will never be a perfect time to make any change. The only aspect that makes any moment better than another is the specific moment when you started to try. The world and life will continue to throw obstacles at you for you to overcome.

Sickness and death will occur. There will be ebbs and flows in the economy. There will be people in your life that are not supportive. The list of potential barriers and obstacles truly can be endless, and we always have the choice and power to add an "and" at the end of the sentence instead of ending it there with a period, or putting a negative spin on with a "but" to emphasize to ourselves that "Yes, this difficult situation is happening, and I have the power and ability to identify the choices I have and move forward from there." It's in this mentality that we are able not only to gain our own sense of self and ability but also to move from victim to survivor. There are many variables when determining how difficult this mind-set shift will be for each one of us at any given moment, yet I can guarantee that it will not be easy. At the very least, I am consistent in my message that change is extremely hard but all the struggle will be worth it in the end. If you truly hate a thought, feeling, action, or situation enough to push through the struggle and discomfort of the unknown and change, then the new place you land will be worth celebrating.

The moment you let go of all of your excuses is the moment when you find freedom. You will tap into all of your inner strength that you have neglected to recognize, even when you have been using it to survive everything life has thrown at you up until this very second. You need to stop and acknowledge this and celebrate it. You have triumphed over every difficult moment and struggle, no matter how large or small, up to this very second. You have gotten over things you did not think you could get over. You have achieved things you never dreamed were possible. It was you, and only you, that carried yourself through each second. No one could have done all of that for you, and no one can do it for you moving forward. It all starts with *you*. The barriers, the ability to plan, the action steps that will be taken, and the motivation that will turn into consistency that will yield the results of your continuous action all start within you with your inner strength. This is the moment that you become unstoppable. You will accept that each step will take time, that it will be hard, and that it will all be worth it. You will start to be more intentional about whom you talk to and spend time with. You will be mindful of which activities you spend the most time doing, and how these fit in with where you are trying to go. You will be able to acknowledge the areas you are still pushing to grow in, and you will seek supports and opportunities to do so. You will start to think about how to make something work instead of just identifying why it will not work. This is what will set you apart from others. This is what will make you stay the course to reach each success marker you set up for yourself. The choice is yours, and yours alone. Choose wisely, because your life depends on it.

Putting Together All the Pieces

When I read or listen to something for the purpose of learning and applying something within my life or work, I always appreciate the notes I took or that were provided to me. I always find a renewed energy and dedication to the process or skill if I have a quick way to have a question answered or clarified when I start to complicate things within my own head. Remember: goal-setting and growing as a person are parts of a life-long journey. If we do not attend formal schooling, that does not mean that we are off the hook when it comes to learning. The responsibility shifts on to us as individuals once we leave school to continue to find opportunities to recall the information we have learned, and to continue to seek out new information. There may not be formal tests, quizzes, and papers to hand in for grades, but the quality of your life and the level at which you can find happiness through your own actions and thoughts will be your report card for how well you are following through. Here are some of the key points and highlights I hope you took away from this process. I am hopeful as well that they will continue to support and inspire you to keep going on your journey of setting and achieving goals, allowing you to pass with flying colors.

A Quick Review of the Process

- Define what you are setting out to achieve so it will be something you can measure and something that is attainable based on what you want to add or subtract from your life to get you closer to feeling happy more often.
- Write this *what* down as your goal in a visible place.
- Define your *why*. This is the reason this goal you are setting is one of the most important things you can spend time focusing on. It should be something that sets your soul ablaze when you think about it.
- Find ways to constantly remind yourself of your *why* to get through the struggles that come from doing something new and challenging.
- Create an outline, or road map, of what will be necessary to make this goal a reality by starting from the finish line of having achieved the goal and working backward to identify not only action steps but also potential barriers that can be planned for.

- This road map will serve as a guide to get started and remain on task, yet it will change over time as you take the necessary steps and are able to get a better assessment of where each step gets you.
- As you take these action steps in your road map, you can use a simple evaluation process after taking each step to decide where that step left you, what you learned, and where you want to go from there—to compare this to your previously developed steps to best know that you are on the right path, or to quickly identify a plan to switch courses in preparation for what is to come next.

Helpful Hints

- Find a way that is most meaningful for you to record these steps that will allow you to access and revise as necessary.
- You should always start with your own desires and wants when it comes to goal-setting, and then assess other people's opinions and feedback. This allows you to be more objective and better filter what is helpful and important feedback versus something that will be a barrier you need to plan for.
- Surround yourself with people that will lift you up and support you in an authentic way. Plan to reciprocate to those in your life and in the world when you are able.
- Remember that asking for support—whether it's a resource, knowledge, or time—from someone is a strength, not a weakness. By not asking, you are limiting your own ability to learn and grow, and robbing the other person's ability to give back and do something that will make him or her feel amazing.

- We control our inner dialogue if we choose to. Learning to identify the messages you send yourself throughout the day, and working to change them to the most helpful messages, will be some of the best time you spend.

- Happiness is experiencing the journey through life and choosing to acknowledge all of the good within that journey instead of focusing only on the negative.

- Feeling every emotion is a gift, and you are in control of the way in which you want to respond to each emotion as you experience it.

- Change is hard, and we often fight against it with every fiber of our being. Yet it is necessary to grow and get to where we are going. Embrace this hard to be able to have the opportunity to celebrate overcoming the challenge and the reward for making the change.

- If you cannot see how you will achieve something from the start, that does not mean it is not achievable. If you believe you can do something, you can find a way to make almost anything happen within the realm of reality.

- Any moment spent on the process of trying to grow and better yourself or a situation is never time wasted. It is when we give up, and never begin again, that we start to fail ourselves.

- Some of your most exciting and life-changing moments may come when you are doing something you never thought you would, or during situations of huge struggle. Focusing on your ability to evaluate your current thoughts and emotions during any moment in life will give you the power to always decide what the next step will be for you.

- The best way to start setting goals is to set small goals for small changes and make them a huge priority. When you start too big, or you try to make many changes all at once, the steps will seem overwhelming and will become a small priority.

- Be patient. Change takes time—especially meaningful change. Trust the process, and give yourself the time and space to experience each piece of the journey as it unfolds. If the process feels slower than you anticipated, or slower than want it to feel, that does not mean that you are not still moving and changing. Small and slow progress is still movement.

Printed in the United States
By Bookmasters